Gaddafi's Harem

Gaddafi's Harem

ANNICK COJEAN

Translated from the French by
Marjolijn de Jager

Grove Press UK

First published in the United States of America in 2013 by Grove/Atlantic Inc.

First published in Great Britain in 2013 by Grove Press UK,
an imprint of Grove/Atlantic Inc.

First published in French in 2013 by Editions Grasset & Fasquelle

1 3 5 7 9 8 6 4 2

A CIP record for this book is available from the British Library.

HB ISBN 978 1 61185 610 1
Ebook ISBN 978 1 61185 981 2

Printed in Italy by Grafica Veneta

Grove Press, UK
Ormond House
26–27 Boswell Street
London
WC1N 3JZ

www.groveatlantic.com

To my mother, always.
To Marie-Gabrielle, Anne, Pipole:
the crucial ones.

*"We in the Jamahiriya and the great revolution affirm
our respect for women and raise their flag. We have decided to
wholly liberate the women of Libya in order to rescue them from
a world of oppression and subjugation in such a way that they will become
masters of their own destiny in a democratic setting where they will have the same
opportunities as the other members of society [...]*

*We call for a revolution to liberate the women of the Arab nation,
which will be a bomb to shake up the entire Arab region, inciting
female prisoners, whether in palaces or marketplaces, to rebel against their
jailers, their exploiters, and their oppressors. This call is certain to
cause profound echoes and repercussions in the entire
Arab nation and in the world at large. Today is not just any day,
it is the beginning of the end of the era of harems and slaves [...]"*

Muammar Gaddafi, September 1, 1981:
the anniversary of the revolution, introducing
the first women to receive diplomas from the
Military Academy for Women

CONTENTS

CONTENTS

PROLOGUE

First, there is Soraya.

Soraya and her dark eyes, her sullen mouth, and her big resounding laugh. Soraya, who moves quick as lightning from laughter to tears, from exuberance to despondency, from cuddly affection to the hostility of the wounded. Soraya and her secret, her sorrow, her rebellion. Soraya and her astonishing story of a joyful little girl thrown into the claws of an ogre.

She is the reason for this book.

I met her in October 2011, on one of those jubilant and chaotic days following the capture and death of the dictator Muammar Gaddafi. I was in Tripoli for the newspaper *Le Monde* investigating the role of women in the revolution. It was a frenzied period and the subject fascinated me.

I was no expert on Libya. In fact, it was my first time visiting the country. I was enthralled by the incredible courage of those fighting to overthrow the tyrant who had ruled for forty-two years, but also genuinely intrigued by the complete

1

absence of women in the films, photographs, and reports that had recently appeared. The other insurrections of the Arab Spring and the wind of hope that had blown across this region of the world had shown the strength of the Tunisian women, present everywhere in public debates, and the confidence and spirit of Egyptian women, whose courage was clear as they demonstrated on Tahrir Square in Cairo. But where were the Libyan women? What had they been doing during the revolution? Was it a revolution they had wanted, initiated, supported? Why were they hiding? Or, more likely, why were they kept from view in this country that was so little known, whose image was monopolized by their buffoon of a leader, who had made the guards of his female corps—the famous Amazons—into the standard-bearers of his own revolution?

Male colleagues who had followed the rebellion from Benghazi to Sirte had told me they'd never come across any women other than a few shadows draped in black veils, since the Libyan fighters had systematically refused them any access to their mothers, wives, or sisters. "Perhaps you'll have better luck!" they said to me with a touch of irony, convinced that in this country history is never written by women, no matter what.

On the first point they were not incorrect. Being a female journalist in the most impenetrable of countries offers the wonderful advantage of having access to the entire society and not just to its men. Consequently, it took me just a few days and many encounters to understand that the role of women in the Libyan revolution had been not only important but, in fact, vital to its success. A man who was one of the rebel leaders told me that women had formed "the secret weapon of the rebellion." They had encouraged, fed, hidden, transported, looked after, and equipped the fighters, as well as providing them with information. They had moved money to purchase arms, spied on Gaddafi's troops on behalf of NATO, redirected tons of medications, including from the hospital run by the adopted daughter of Muammar Gaddafi (the same one he—untruthfully—said had died after the Americans bombed his residence in 1986). These women had risked unbelievable things: arrest, torture, and rape. Rape—considered to be the worst of all crimes in Libya—was common practice and an authorized weapon of war. They had committed themselves body and soul to this revolution. They were fanatic, spectacular, heroic. "Women had a personal account to settle with the Colonel," one of them told me.

A "personal account" . . . I didn't immediately understand the significance of this remark. Having just endured four decades of dictatorship, didn't every Libyan have a *communal* account to settle with the despot? The confiscation of individual rights and liberties, the bloody repression of opponents, the deterioration of the health and education systems, the disastrous state of the country's infrastructure, the impoverishment of the population, the collapse of culture, the misappropriation of oil profits, and the isolation on the international stage . . . why then this "personal account" of women? Had the author of the *Green Book* not endlessly proclaimed that men and women were equal? Had he not systematically presented himself as their fierce defender, raising the legal age for marriage to twenty, condemning polygamy and the abuses of the patriarchal society, granting more rights to divorced women than existed in most other Muslim countries, and founding a Military Academy for Women open to candidates from all over the world? "Nonsense, hypocrisy, travesty!" a famous woman judge would later tell me. "We were all his potential prey."

It was at that same time that I first met Soraya. Our paths crossed the morning of October 29. I was completing my investigation and was ready to leave Tripoli the next day to go back to Paris, via Tunisia. I was sorry to be going home. Although, admittedly, I had obtained an answer to my first question, concerning women's participation in the revolution, and was returning with a whole supply of stories and detailed accounts that illustrated their struggle, so many questions remained unanswered. The rapes perpetrated en masse by Gaddafi's mercenaries and troops were an insurmountable taboo, locking authorities, families, and women's organizations inside a hostile silence. The International Criminal Court, which had launched an investigation into these rapes, was itself confronted with terrible difficulties when its lawyers tried to meet with the victims. As for the sufferings that women endured before the revolution, these were brought up only as rumors, accompanied by many deep sighs and furtive glances. "What's the use of bringing up such vile and unforgivable practices and crimes?" I'd often hear. Never a first-person testimony. Not even the slightest story from a victim that might implicate the so-called Guide.

But then Soraya arrived. She was wearing a black shawl covering a mass of thick hair pulled into a bun, large sunglasses, and loosely flowing pants. Full lips gave her the appearance of an Angelina Jolie look-alike, and when she smiled a childlike spark lit up her face, which was beautiful even though already etched by life. "How old do you think I am?" she asked as she took off her glasses. She waited, anxiously, and then spoke before I could answer: "I feel like I'm forty-two!" To her that was old—she was just twenty-two.

It was a brilliant day in Tripoli, a city on edge. Muammar Gaddafi had been dead for more than a week; the National Transitional Council had officially declared the country's liberation; and Green Square, rebaptized to its former name, the Square of the Martyrs, had seen another crowd of euphoric Tripoli inhabitants come together the previous night, chanting the names of Allah and Libya in a performance of revolutionary songs and bursts of Kalashnikov fire. Each city district had bought a camel and slaughtered it in front of a mosque, sharing it with refugees from towns that had been devastated in the war. They said they were "united" and "in solidarity," "happier than they could ever remember being." They were also worn out, completely spent. Incapable of going back to work and picking up the normal routine. Libya without Gaddafi . . . it was unimaginable.

Gaudy vehicles kept on crossing the city, discharging rebels from hoods, roofs, and car doors, flags blowing in the wind. The drivers were honking, each brandishing a weapon like a treasured girlfriend you might take to a party. They were shouting "Allahu Akbar," embracing, making the V for Victory sign, a red-black-and-green scarf tied around his head pirate style or worn as an armband, and never mind the fact that not every last one of them had fought from the first moment on or with the same courage. Since the fall of Sirte, the Guide's last bastion, and his immediate execution, everyone was declaring himself a rebel.

Soraya was looking at them from a distance and feeling depressed.

Was it the atmosphere of rowdy joy that made the malaise she'd felt since the Guide's death more bitter? Was it the glorification of the revolution's "martyrs" and "heroes" that took her back to her sad status of secret, unwanted, shameful victim? Did the revolution make her appraise the disaster of her life thus far? She had no words for it, was unable to explain it. All she felt was the burning sense of utter injustice. The anguish of being unable to express her grief and howl her rebellion. The terror of having her wretchedness, unheard of in Libya and much too difficult to explain, summarily dismissed. It wasn't possible. It wasn't right.

She was nibbling at her shawl, nervously covering the lower half of her face. Tears appeared on her cheeks, but she quickly wiped them away. "Muammar Gaddafi ruined my life," she said. She had to talk—the memories were too much to bear silently. "I have scars," she said, scars that were causing her nightmares. "No matter what I say, no one will ever know where I come from or what I've been through. No one could ever imagine. No one." She shook her head in despair. "When I saw Gaddafi's body displayed to the crowd I felt a brief moment of pleasure. Then I had a terrible taste in my mouth. I had wanted him to live. To be captured and put on trial, to be judged by an international court. I wanted him to account for his actions."

For Soraya was a victim. One of those victims that Libyan society doesn't want to hear about. One of those victims whose dishonor and humiliation reflect on the whole family and the entire nation. One of those victims who are so disturbing and unsettling that it's easier to make them the culprits. Guilty of having been victimized . . . With all of the strength a twenty-two-year-old girl could muster, Soraya energetically refused this. She dreamed of justice. She wanted to testify. What had been done to her and to so many others seemed to her neither innocuous nor forgivable. What was her story? She was about to tell it: the story of a barely fifteen-year-old girl whom Muammar Gaddafi noticed during a visit to her school and abducted the following day to become his sexual slave, together with other young girls.

Imprisoned for several years inside the fortified residence of Bab al-Azizia, she was beaten, raped, and exposed to every perversion of a sex-obsessed tyrant. He had robbed her of her virginity and her youth, thereby preventing her from having any kind of respectable future in Libya's society. She was bitterly aware of it. After weeping and lamenting over her situation, her family ultimately decided that she was no more than a slut. Beyond redemption. She smoked, never went out anymore, didn't know where to go. I was speechless.

I returned to France shattered by Soraya's story and reported it in an article in *Le Monde,* without revealing either her face or her identity. That would be too dangerous; they had already made her suffer enough. But then the story was picked up and translated all over the world. It was the first time that an account from one of the young women of that mysterious place of Bab al-Azizia had been circulated. Pro-Gaddafi websites denied it vehemently, indignant that the image of their alleged hero, who had done so much for the "liberation" of women, should be thus vilified. Although they had no illusions about the mores of the Guide, others considered it so horrifying that they had trouble believing it. The international media tried to find Soraya, but in vain.

I didn't doubt her story for a second, as very similar tales that proved the existence of many other Sorayas were reaching me. I learned that hundreds of young women had been abducted for an hour, a night, a week, or years, and been forced to submit to Gaddafi's sexual fantasies and violence by force or through blackmail; that he had networks available to him involving diplomats, military men, bodyguards, employees of the administration and the so-called Department of Protocol whose central mission it was to provide their master with young women—or young men—for his daily consumption. I learned that fathers and husbands would keep their daughters and wives confined in order to keep them away from the eyes and lust of the Guide. I found out that, born into a family of extremely poor Bedouins, Gaddafi was a tyrant who ruled through sex, obsessed with the idea of one day possessing the wives or daughters of the rich and powerful, of his ministers and generals, of chiefs of state and monarchs. He was prepared to pay the price. Any price. For him there were no limits whatsoever.

But the new Libya isn't ready to talk of this. Taboo! However, no one hesitates to pour scorn on Gaddafi and to demand that light be shed on his forty-two years of depravity and absolute power. They list the physical abuse of political prisoners, the atrocities committed against opponents, the tortures and murders of rebels. They tirelessly condemn his tyranny and corruption, his deception and madness, his manipulations and perversions. And they insist on reparation for victims. But no one wants to hear about the hundreds of young girls whom he enslaved and raped. Those girls should just disappear or emigrate, wrapped in a veil, their grief bundled up inside a bag. The simplest thing yet would be for them to die. And some of the men in their families are prepared to take care of that.

I returned to Libya to see Soraya again. I collected other stories and tried to probe the networks of those under the tyrant's heel. It would prove to be a high-pressure investigation. Victims and witnesses are still living in terror of tackling the subject. Some are the target of threats and intimidation. "For the sake of Libya, and for your own sake, drop this investigation!" some people advised me before abruptly hanging up the phone. And from his prison in Misrata, where he now spends his days reading the Koran, a bearded young man—who participated in trafficking young girls—told me in exasperation: "Gaddafi is dead! Dead! Why do you want to dig up his shameful secrets?" The minister of defense, Oussama Jouili, had a very similar position: "It's a matter of national shame and humiliation. When I think of the affronts perpetrated on so many young people, soldiers included, I feel nothing but disgust! I assure you, the best thing to do is to keep quiet. The Libyans feel collectively tainted and want to turn the page."

So there are crimes to be condemned and others to be camouflaged like dirty little secrets? Some victims are good and noble and others are ignominious? There are those who must be honored, favored, recompensed, and those on whom it is critical to "turn the page"? No. That is unacceptable. Soraya's story is not an anecdote. Crimes against women—treated so casually, not to say complacently, throughout the world—are not a trivial matter.

Soraya's story is courageous and should be read as a testimony, a historical document. I wrote it as she dictated it to me. She is eloquent, has an excellent memory, and cannot bear the thought of a conspiracy of silence. There is undoubtedly no criminal court that will one day bring her justice. Perhaps Libya will never even recognize the suffering of Muammar Gaddafi's "prey" under a system that was created in his image. But, at least, while he was strutting about at the UN as if he were the master of the universe, while other nations rolled out the red carpet for him and welcomed him with great fanfare, while his Amazons were a subject of curiosity, fascination, or amusement, her testimony will be there to prove that at home, in his vast residence of Bab al-Azizia—or rather in its humid basements—Muammar Gaddafi was holding captive young girls who were still only children when they arrived.

PART ONE
SORAYA'S STORY

1

CHILDHOOD

I was born in Marag, a small town in the region of Djebel Akhdar—the Green Mountain—not far from the Egyptian border, on February 17, 1989. Yes, February 17! It's impossible for Libyans not to understand the significance of that date: it's the day the revolution that ousted Gaddafi from power began in 2011. In other words, it's a day that's destined to become a national holiday, and that pleases me.

Three brothers came before me, and two more were born after me, as well as my little sister. But I was the first girl, which made my father wild with joy. He so wanted a girl. He wanted a Soraya. He'd thought of that name well before he was married. And he often told me how he felt when he saw me for the first time: "You were so pretty! So very pretty!" He was so elated that on the seventh day after my birth the customary celebration was as grand as a wedding party. The house was full of guests, music, a large buffet. He wanted everything for his daughter—the same opportunities, the same chances in life, the same rights as my brothers had. Even today he says that he had dreamed I would become a doctor. And it's true that he made me register for natural science courses in secondary school. Had my life followed a normal course maybe I really would have studied medicine. Who knows? But don't talk to me about having the same chances in life as my brothers. You can forget that! There's not a Libyan woman alive who would believe that. All you need to do is see how my mother, despite her being so modern, ended up having to abandon most of her dreams.

Her dreams were boundless, and now all of them are broken. She was born in Morocco at the home of her grand-mother, whom she adored. But her parents were Tunisian. She had a great deal of freedom because as a young girl she went to Paris to be trained as a hairdresser. A real dream, right? That's where she met Papa, at a big dinner one night during Ramadan. He was working for the country's foreign informa-tion service and spending long periods of time at the Libyan Embassy. He, too, loved Paris. The atmosphere was so light-hearted, so joyful, compared to the oppressive Libyan climate. He could have taken courses at the Alliance Française, as acquaintances had suggested, but he was too carefree and pre-ferred going out, wandering around, grabbing every minute of freedom he could manage. Today he regrets not being able to speak French. It would certainly have changed our life. In any event, as soon as he met Mama he quickly made up his mind. He asked for her hand, and the wedding took place in Fez, where her grandmother still lived, and then presto, all smug, he took her back with him to Libya.

What a shock for my mother! She never imagined she'd be living in the Middle Ages. She who was so chic, so careful to be stylish, well coiffed, well made-up, she now had to drape herself in the traditional white veil and keep her outings to a minimum. She was like a caged tiger. She felt cheated and trapped. It was nothing like the life that Papa had made her believe she'd have. He'd talked about traveling between France and Libya, about her work, which she could develop while going from one country to the other. Within days of getting married, she found herself in the land of the Bedouins. She became depressed. So Papa moved the family to Benghazi, the second largest city in Libya, in the eastern part of the country. A provincial town, but still considered to be a little anti-authoritarian compared to the power in Tripoli. He couldn't take her to Paris, a city he himself still continued to visit, but at least she'd be living in a large city and could develop her family business. As if the hair salon could console her!

Mama kept on brooding and dreaming of Paris. To us little ones she spoke of her walks on the Champs-Elysées, having tea with her women friends on café terraces. She would talk about the freedom that French women had, and also of the social welfare system, labor union rights, the boldness of the press.

Paris, Paris, Paris. In the end this kind of talk bored us kids. But it made my father feel guilty. He had envisioned starting a small business in Paris, a restaurant in the fifteenth arrondissement, which Mama could have run. Sadly, he soon had a fight with his business partner and the project fell apart. At the time, he almost bought an apartment in the Défense area for twenty-five thousand dollars, but he didn't want to take the risk and still regrets that, now that it has become one of the city's most exclusive neighborhoods.

So my earliest school memories are from Benghazi. They are already a bit blurry but I do recall that it was a happy time. The school's name was the Lion Cubs of the Revolution and I had four girlfriends there; we were inseparable. I was the comedian of the group—my specialty was imitating the teachers as soon as they left the classroom, or mimicking the principal. It seems I have a gift for capturing people's looks and expressions. We five would cry with laughter together. I had an F in math but was the best of my class in Arabic.

Papa wasn't earning much and Mama's work became indispensable. In fact, the family's finances soon depended on her. She was working day and night, living in the hope that something would happen to take us far away from Libya. I knew she was different from other mothers and at school they'd sometimes treat me disdainfully as "the daughter of that Tunisian woman." That hurt. Tunisian women had the reputation of being modern, emancipated, and in Benghazi those were not considered to be fine qualities. Foolishly, the fact that my mother was Tunisian upset me. I almost held it against my father that he hadn't chosen a wife from his own country. Why did he need to marry a foreigner? Had he given any thought to his children? My God, how stupid I was!

The year I turned eleven, Papa announced that we were moving to Sirte, a city between Benghazi and Tripoli, also on the Mediterranean coast. He wanted to be closer to his birthplace, to his father—a highly traditional man with four wives—as well as to his brothers and cousins. That's how it is in Libya. Every family member tries to stay close to home—that supposedly gives them strength and unconditional support. In Benghazi, without roots or relations, we were like orphans. Or so, at least, Papa explained it to us. But I myself took this news as a complete catastrophe. Leave my school? My friends? What a disaster! It made me sick. Physically sick. I was in bed for two weeks, incapable of getting up to go to the new school.

But in the end I went. With lead in my shoes and knowing all too soon that I wasn't going to be happy there. First of all, you need to understand that we were moving to Gaddafi's birthplace. I haven't mentioned him yet because at home he was neither a concern nor a frequent topic of conversation. Mama clearly detested him. She'd change channels as soon as he appeared on television. She called him "the unkempt one" and, shaking her head, she'd ask repeatedly: "Honestly now, does that guy really have the face of a president?" I think Papa was afraid of talking this way about Gaddafi, so he'd remain silent. We all sensed intuitively that the less we spoke of him the better it was, since the slightest mention of him outside the family circle might be reported and cause us a great deal of trouble. So we had no photograph of him in our house, and weren't involved in anything the least bit political. Let's just say that instinctively we were all very cautious.

At school, on the other hand, it was pure adoration. His image was everywhere; every morning we'd sing the national anthem in front of an immense poster of him, which was attached to the green flag; and we'd cry: "You are our Guide, we walk behind You, blah blah blah"; and in class or during recess, students would talk with pure adulation about the man they referred to as "my cousin Muammar," "my uncle Muammar," while the teachers spoke of him as a demigod. No, as a god. He was good; he watched over his children; he was all-powerful. We all had to call him "Papa Muammar." To us he seemed gigantic.

Although we moved to Sirte to be closer to the family and feel more integrated in a community, things didn't work out this way. Basking in the glow of their blood relationship or connection to Gaddafi, the people of Sirte felt they were the masters of the world. Let's just say that, when confronted with the hicks and boors from other towns, they felt like aristocrats, regulars at the court. You're from Zliten? How gross! From Benghazi? Ridiculous. From Tunisia? Embarrassing!

No matter what she did, Mama was truly a source of disgrace. And when she opened a nice-looking hair salon in the center of town not far from our building in Dubai Street, the contempt for her only increased, though the elegant women of Sirte still came running. My mother was really talented. Everyone recognized her skill in creating the finest hairdos in the city and doing fabulous makeup. I'm quite sure that she was envied. But you have no idea how repressed Sirte is through its traditionalism and prudishness. A woman without a veil can be insulted on the streets. And even with a veil she is suspect. What in the world is she doing outside? She must be looking for an adventure or maybe she's having an affair. People spy on one another, neighbors watch the comings and goings of the house across from them, families are jealous of each other, protect their daughters, and gossip about everyone else. The tattletales are working around the clock.

So at school it was double trouble. Not only was I the daughter of "that Tunisian woman," but I was also "the girl from the salon." They put me at a desk all by myself, apart from the other students. And I never managed to have a Libyan girlfriend. Fortunately, after a while I became friendly with the daughter of a Libyan man and a Palestinian woman. Then with a Moroccan girl and then with the daughter of a Libyan and an Egyptian woman. But never with any of the local girls. Even when I lied one day and said my mother was Moroccan, which seemed less serious to me than being from Tunisia. But, no, it was worse. So basically my life revolved around the hair salon. It became my kingdom.

I'd run over there as soon as classes were over—and it was there that I came back to life after school. It was so wonderful!

First of all because I was helping Mama and that was a delightful feeling, but also because I liked the work. My mother never stopped and, although she had four employees, she was constantly running from one customer to the next. They did hair, makeup, and skin treatments. And I can assure you that in Sirte, although the women may well be hiding beneath a veil, they're still exceedingly demanding and incredibly sophisticated. I specialized in removing hair from the face and eyebrows, using a silk thread that I'd wind between my fingers and manipulate very fast to catch the hair. Much better than tweezers or wax. I'd also prepare women's faces for the application of makeup, putting on the foundation, after which my mother would take over, working on the eyes before calling for me, saying: "Soraya! The final touch!" And I'd come running to apply lipstick, to check the total result, and to add a dab of perfume.

The salon soon became the meeting place for the city's elegant women. Meaning the women of the Gaddafi clan, as well. When there were important international summits taking place in Sirte, the women of the different delegations would come to be made beautiful, including the wives of African presidents and of European and American heads of state. It's strange, but I especially remember the wife of the leader of Nicaragua, who wanted us to draw huge eyes for her below her enormous chignon. One day, one of Gaddafi's bodyguards, a man called Judia, came to pick up Mama by car to do the hair and makeup of the Guide's wife. It proved that Mama had acquired quite a reputation! So off she went. She spent several hours taking care of Safia Gaddafi, and was paid a ludicrous sum of money, way below her usual fee. She was furious and felt really humiliated. So when Judia returned later on to take her back there again, she quite simply refused, claiming to have too much work to do. Other times she actually hid, leaving me to explain that she wasn't there. She really has character, my mother. She never gave an inch.

The women of the Gaddafi clan were generally insufferable. If I'd go up to one of them to ask whether she wanted to have her hair styled or dyed, she'd say contemptuously: "And who exactly are you to be addressing me?" One morning one of them, elegant and gorgeous, came into the salon, and I was fascinated with her. "How beautiful you are!" I said spontaneously. She slapped me. Petrified at first, I ran to Mama, who muttered between her teeth: "Be quiet. The customer is always right." Three months later I saw the same lady open the door of the salon. She came toward me, said that her daughter who was my age had just died of cancer, and apologized to me. That was even more startling than her slap.

Another time, a bride-to-be reserved the salon for the day of her wedding and put down a small deposit but then canceled. Mama refused to reimburse her, and she turned into a real she-devil. She started shrieking and breaking everything in sight, then alerted the Gaddafi clan, which arrived in full force and wrecked the salon. One of my brothers came to the rescue and was beaten up. When the police intervened it was my brother who ended up in jail. The Gaddafis did everything to keep him there as long as possible, and it took lengthy negotiating between the tribes to reach an agreement, which was followed by an official pardon. He was set free six months later, his skull shaved and his body covered with bruises. He had been tortured. And the tribal agreement notwithstanding, the Gaddafis, who ran every institution in Sirte, including city hall, joined forces to keep the salon closed for another month. I was appalled.

My oldest brother, Nasser, scared me a little and always took an authoritarian role toward me. But Aziz, just a year older than I, was almost like a twin to me, a real partner. Since we attended the same school, I felt he was both protective and jealous. And I served as a go-between for a few of his infatuations. I myself wasn't thinking about love. Not at all. That page was blank. Perhaps, knowing that my mother was strict and very severe, I was censoring myself. I have no idea. I didn't indulge in the slightest crush, not the smallest thrill, the most distant dream. I think that for the rest of my life I'll regret never having had a childhood sweetheart. I knew that I'd get married someday since that is every woman's destiny, and that I would then have to use makeup and be beautiful for my husband. But I knew nothing else. Not about my body, not about sexuality. I was in a panic when I got my period! I went running to tell my mother but she didn't explain a thing to me. And I began to feel ashamed when a commercial for sanitary napkins appeared on TV. Suddenly embarrassed to see these images in the presence of the boys in the family. I remember Mama and my aunts saying to me: "When you're eighteen we'll tell you a few things." What things? "Life." But they never had a chance to explain anything to me. Muammar Gaddafi was ahead of them. And he destroyed me.

One April morning in 2004—I had just turned fifteen—the high school principal addressed all the students gathered in the courtyard: "The Guide is doing us the great honor of paying us a visit tomorrow. This is a thrill for the entire school. So I am counting on you to be on time, to be orderly, and to be well dressed. You are to present the image of a magnificent school, the way he likes it and deserves to see it!" What a piece of news! What a story! You can't imagine the excitement. To see Gaddafi in person . . . His face had been known to me since I was born. His photographs were everywhere—on city walls, in administrative buildings, in town halls, at businesses. On T-shirts, necklaces, notebooks. Not to mention the banknotes. We were living permanently under his gaze, living in his personality cult. And in spite of Mama's acerbic remarks, I nursed a timid reverence for him. I couldn't even imagine his life, since I thought he was more than human. He was above the fray, on an inaccessible Olympus where purity reigned.

So the next day, in a meticulously ironed uniform—black pants and tunic, a white scarf around my face—I ran to school, impatiently waiting to be told how the day would unfold. But the first class had hardly started when a teacher came to get me, saying that I'd been chosen to present the Guide with flowers and gifts. Me! The girl from the salon! The student they kept away from the rest! I was completely in shock. First I opened my eyes wide in disbelief, then I got up, radiant and conscious of the envy of many of the girls in my class. They brought me to a large room with a handful of students who'd also been selected and ordered us to quickly change into traditional Libyan dress. The clothes were there, on hangers. Red tunic, red pants, a veil, and a little hat that they placed carefully on our hair. How exciting it all was! The teachers hurried us along, adjusting our veils, pinning our clothes, smoothing down our unruly locks with a hair dryer. I asked: "Tell me how to greet him, I beg you! What am I supposed to do? Bow down before him? Kiss his hand? Recite something?" My heart was beating a hundred miles a minute while everyone worked hard to make us look magnificent. As I think back to that scene today, I see it as preparing lambs to be led to slaughter.

The school auditorium was packed. Teachers, students, administrators—everyone was nervously waiting. We, the small group of girls meant to welcome the Guide, were lined up in front of the entrance and were exchanging meaningful glances, as if to say: "Really, what luck! We'll remember this moment for the rest of our lives!" I clutched my bouquet of flowers and was shaking like a leaf. My legs felt like rubber. One teacher cast a stern look at me and said, "Come on, Soraya, stand up straight!"

And suddenly, there He was. Cameras flashed as he came out, surrounded by a horde of people and female bodyguards. He was wearing a white uniform, his chest covered with insignia, flags, and decorations, a beige shawl over his shoulders that matched the color of the small cap on his head from which some dark black hair peaked out. It all happened very fast. I held out the bouquet, then took his free hand in mine and kissed it as I bowed down. That's when I felt him squeezing my palm in a strange manner. Then he looked me over coldly, from top to bottom. He pressed my shoulder, placed a hand on my head, and patted my hair. And there my life ended. For, as I later learned, that gesture was a sign to the bodyguards that meant: "That's the one I want!"

But at that moment I felt like I was on a cloud. As soon as the visit came to an end, I flew rather than ran to the hair salon to tell my mother all about it. "Papa Muammar smiled at me, Mama. I swear he did! He patted my head!" To be honest, what I remembered was a rather icy grin, but I was bubbling over and wanted everyone to know about it. "Don't make such a big deal of it!" Mama said, and continued to pull out curlers from the hair of one of her customers.

"But really, Mama! He's the leader of Libya! That's not just anything, after all!"

"Oh yeah? He threw this country back into the Middle Ages; he's dragging his people into the abyss! You call that a leader?"

I was disgusted and went home to relish my euphoria by myself. Papa was in Tripoli, but my brothers did seem fairly amazed. Except for my brother Aziz, who was not at all happy about it.

When I returned to school the next morning I noticed a radical change in the teachers' attitude. Usually they were brusque, even scornful toward me, but now they were almost affectionate, or at least considerate. When one of them called me "my little Soraya" I raised my eyebrows, and when another asked "So you're going back to class?" as if it were an *option,* I figured something was out of the ordinary. But as it was only one day after the event I gave it no further thought. At one o'clock, the end of the school day, I dashed home to change, and at one-thirty I was in the hair salon to help Mama.

Close to three in the afternoon, Gaddafi's women opened the door. Faiza first, then Salma, and Mabrouka last. Salma was in her bodyguard uniform, with a gun on her belt. The others were wearing traditional dress. They looked around—it was a busy day—and asked one of the employees "Where is Soraya's mother?" and then walked straight up to her.

"We belong to the Committee of the Revolution and were with Muammar yesterday morning when he visited the school. Soraya caught his attention. She looked superb in her traditional dress and conducted herself beautifully. The Committee wishes for her to present another bouquet to Papa Muammar, so she is to come with us immediately."

"But now is a really inconvenient time! As you can see, the salon is full of clients and I need my daughter here!"

"It won't take more than an hour."

"Is it really only a matter of presenting some flowers?"

"She might have to do the makeup of some of the women in the Guide's entourage."

"In that case, it's different. I should go there myself!"

"No, no! Soraya must present the bouquet."

I was present during this conversation, intrigued at first and soon very excited. It was true that Mama was overwhelmed that particular day, but I felt a bit embarrassed that she was so obvious in her reluctance. If it was the Guide's wish, one really couldn't say no, after all! In the end my mother acquiesced—she didn't have any choice—and I followed the three women. A huge 4x4 was parked in front of the shop. The driver started the motor before we'd even sat down, with Mabrouka in the front and me in the back squashed between Salma and Faiza. We shot off at high speed, followed by two cars I immediately noticed. Without knowing it then, I was saying farewell to my childhood.

2

PRISONER

We drove for quite a while. I had no idea of the time but it seemed interminable. We'd left Sirte and were tearing through the desert. I was looking straight ahead, not daring to ask any questions. And then we arrived in Sdadah, in a kind of encampment. There were several tents, more 4x4s, and an immense trailer, or rather an extremely luxurious camper van. Mabrouka headed for the vehicle, motioning me to follow her, and in another car that was turning back I thought I noticed one of the girls from school who'd also been chosen to welcome the Guide the previous day. That should have reassured me, and yet the moment I entered the camper an unspeakable sense of dread grabbed hold of me. As if my entire being was fighting against the situation. As if it knew intuitively that something very bad was being hatched.

Muammar Gaddafi was inside, sitting on a red massage chair, holding a remote control. He looked imperial. I took a step forward to kiss his hand, which he extended halfheartedly while looking away. "Where are Faiza and Salma?" he asked Mabrouka in an irritated voice. "They're coming." I was dumbfounded. Not even a glance at me. I didn't exist. Several minutes went by; I didn't know what to do with myself. He finally stood up and asked: "Where is your family from?"

"From Zliten."

His face remained expressionless. "Get her ready!" he commanded, and left the room. Mabrouka motioned for me to sit down on a bench in a corner of the room, which was set up to look like a living room. The other two women came in, at ease, as if they were at home. Faiza smiled at me, approached me, and unceremoniously held on to my chin. "Don't you worry, little Soraya!" she said, and then laughed and quickly left. Mabrouka was on the phone giving instructions for someone's arrival, perhaps another girl like me, since I heard her say: "Bring her here."

She hung up and turned to me: "Come! We're going to take your measurements to get you some clothes. What is your bra size?" I was stunned. "I . . . I don't know. Mama always buys me my clothes." She looked annoyed and called Fatiha, another woman—well, actually, a strange person who had the voice and shoulders of a man but the imposing bust of a woman. She sized me up, then patted my hand and gave me a big wink. "So this is the new one? And where does this one

31

come from?" She put a measuring tape around my waist and my chest, pressing hers beneath my chin. Then they wrote down my measurements and left the camper. I remained all alone, not daring to call out or move. Night was falling, and I didn't have a clue. What would Mama think? Had they alerted her to the delay? What was going to happen here? And how would I be getting home?

After long minutes of waiting, Mabrouka reappeared. I was relieved to see her. She took me by the arm without a word and led me to a corner lab, where a blonde nurse took my blood. Then Fatiha dragged me to a bathroom. "Get undressed. You're hairy. We need to get rid of all that." She rubbed a depilatory cream on my arms and legs, then shaved me, adding: "We're leaving the pubic hair." I was nonplussed and embarrassed but, since I had to make some sort of sense of it all, I told myself it must be a hygiene thing for anyone who was to come near the Guide. They wrapped me in a robe and I went back to the living room. Mabrouka and Salma—the gun still on her belt—sat down near me.

"We're going to dress you properly, put makeup on, and then you'll be able to see Papa Muammar."

"All this just to greet Papa Muammar? And when am I going home to my parents?"

"Later! First you have to greet your master."

They handed me a G-string—something I'd never seen before—and a white satiny dress, slit at the sides and low-cut at the neck and back. My hair, now loosened, came down to my bottom. Fatiha applied makeup and perfume, then added a bit of gloss to my lips, something that Mama would never have allowed me to do. With a sternly critical eye, Mabrouka inspected the result. Then she took me by the hand and led me down the hall. She stopped in front of a door, opened it, and pushed me in.

Gaddafi was on his bed, naked. I was terrified. I covered my eyes and shrank back in shock, thinking: "There's been a horrible mistake! I'm not meant to be here now. Oh, my God!" I turned around and saw Mabrouka there on the threshold, her expression unrelenting. "He's not dressed!" I muttered, completely panic-stricken and thinking that Mabrouka must not have realized this. "Go in!" she said, pushing me back inside. Then he grabbed my hand and forced me to sit down on the bed beside him. I didn't dare look at him. "Turn around, you whore!"

That word. I didn't really know what it meant but I sensed it was an awful word, a vulgar word, a word for a despicable woman. I didn't budge. He tried to turn me toward him but I resisted. He pulled my arm, my shoulder. My whole body stiffened. Then he forced me to move my head by pulling at my hair. "Don't be afraid. I am your Papa—that's what you call me, isn't it? But I am your brother as well, and soon I'll be your lover. I'll be all of that to you. Because you're going to stay here and be with me forever." His face came close to mine—I could smell his breath. He began to kiss me on my neck, my cheeks. I remained as stiff as a piece of wood. He wanted to embrace me but I moved away. He approached me, but I turned from him and began to cry. He went to grab my head. I leaped up, he pulled my arm, and I pushed him away, so he got irritated, wanted to force me to lie down, and we got into a struggle. He was growling.

Mabrouka appeared. "Look at this whore!" he yelled to her. "She refuses to do what I want! Teach her! Educate her! And then bring her back to me!"

He headed for a small bathroom next to the bedroom as Mabrouka dragged me to the lab. She was white with rage.

"How dare you behave like that with your master? It is your duty to obey him!"

"I want to go home."

"You're not budging! Your place is here!"

"Give me my things, I want to go see Mama."

She slapped me across the face, which made me reel. "Obey! Or else Muammar will make you pay for it very dearly!" My hand on my burning cheek, I looked at her, baffled. "You pretend you're an innocent little girl, you hypocrite, but you know perfectly well what's going on! From now on you will listen to us, to Papa Muammar and to me. And you will do what we tell you. Without a word of complaint, you understand?"

Then she disappeared, leaving me by myself in that flimsy little dress, my makeup smudged and my hair all over the place. I curled up into a ball in the living room and cried for hours. I didn't understand a thing, nothing at all. It was all too perplexing. What was I doing here? What did they want from me? I thought about how Mama must be worried to death, how she must have phoned Papa in Tripoli; perhaps he'd even returned to Sirte. He would be bombarding her with accusations for having let me leave—he never let me leave the house. But how could I ever tell them about that ghastly scene with Papa Muammar? My father would go crazy. I was still shaking with sobs when a blonde nurse, whom I shall never forget, sat down beside me and gently caressed my face. "Tell me what happened," she said. She spoke with a foreign accent, and I later found out she was one of the Guide's Ukrainian nurses, and that her name was Galina. I wasn't able to say a word to her, but she guessed and I could tell she was furious. "How could they do that to a little girl? How dare they?" she kept repeating as she lightly touched my face.

I finally fell asleep, and it was Mabrouka who woke me up the next morning around nine. She handed me a jogging outfit and I began to have some hope again.

"So I'm going home now?"

"I told you no! Are you deaf? I told you very clearly that your old life is finished once and for all. Your parents have been told, and they understood, so why can't you?"

"You phoned my parents?"

I was shattered. I gulped down some tea, nibbled at a cookie, and looked around. Lots of girls in soldiers' uniforms were coming in and going out, glancing at me with curiosity— "Is that the new one?"—and talking about the Guide, who was apparently busy in a tent. Salma approached me. "I'm going to make some things clear to you: Muammar is going to sleep with you. He's going to open you. From here on in you will be his possession and you'll never leave him. So stop making that face. It's no use resisting or wishing things were different—that won't change anything here!"

Then that woman Fatiha came in, turned on the television, and whispered to me: "Let them do what they want with you, that'll make it a lot easier. If you don't resist, you'll be fine. You just have to do everything that's asked of you."

I cried and lay there motionless. So I was a prisoner. What could I have possibly done wrong?

Around one o'clock Fatiha came to dress me in a very short blue satin dress; actually, it was more like a negligee. In the bathroom she wet my hair and then puffed it out with some mousse. Mabrouka checked my appearance, took me firmly by the hand, and once again led me to Gaddafi's bedroom. "This time you'll satisfy your master's desires or else I'll kill you!" she threatened, then opened the door and pushed me in. There he was, the Guide, sitting on his bed in jogging pants and an undershirt, a cigarette in his mouth, as he slowly blew out smoke while looking at me coldly. "You're a whore," he said. "Your mother is Tunisian, which makes you a whore." He was taking his time, looking me over from top to bottom and back up again, and blowing smoke at me. "Sit down, close to me," and he pointed to a spot on the bed. "You're going to do everything I ask you to do. I'll give you jewelry and a beautiful house, I'll teach you how to drive and give you a car. One day you may even be able to study abroad if you want. I will take you wherever you want to go. Do you hear what I'm saying? Your every wish will be fulfilled!"

"I want to go home to Mama."

He froze, put out his cigarette, and raised his voice.

"Listen to me carefully! Stop that, you hear? Stop that business about going home. From now on you'll be here with me! And you must forget everything else!"

I couldn't believe what he was saying. It was beyond all comprehension. He pulled me to the bed and bit me on my upper arm. It hurt. Then he tried to undress me. I already felt so naked in that tiny blue minidress; it was horrible—I couldn't let him undress me. I resisted, clinging to the straps. "Take it off, dirty whore!" He pulled my arms apart; I stood up; he caught me again and flung me on the bed; I struggled. Then he got up in a rage and disappeared into the bathroom. Mabrouka was there in a second. (I found out only later that he had a little bell near the bed with which to call her.)

"This is the first time any girl has resisted me like this! It's your fault, Mabrouka! I told you to teach her! So get it done or you'll pay the price!"

"My master, forget this girl! She's stubborn as a mule. We'll throw her back to her mother and I'll find you some others."

"No, get this one ready! It's her I want!"

They brought me back to the lab, where I stayed, there in the dark. Galina slipped in for a moment and with a pitying

37

look gave me a blanket. But how could I sleep? I was reliving what had just happened, trying to find an explanation for what I was going through. What had they told my parents? Surely not the truth, that wasn't possible. But what, then? Papa didn't even let me go to the neighbors' and always told me to be home before dark. So what was he thinking, what ideas could he have? Would they believe me when someday I told them what had happened? What explanation had they given to my school when I didn't show up? I didn't sleep at all that night. At dawn, just as I was beginning to pass out from exhaustion, Mabrouka came in. "Up you get! Put on this uniform. We're leaving for Sirte."

Oh, what a relief! "So we're going home to Mama?"

"No, somewhere else!"

At least we were leaving this horrible place in the middle of nowhere and going closer to home. I hurriedly washed, put on my khaki uniform, which resembled the clothes of Gaddafi's bodyguards, and went back to the living room, where five other girls, also in uniform, were absentmindedly watching television. They were holding cell phones and I was dying to ask them to call Mama but Mabrouka had her eyes on me and the atmosphere was glacial. The camper van pulled away. I let myself be carried off—it had been a long time since I'd had any control over anything.

About an hour later the vehicle stopped. They made us get out and then split us up in different cars, by fours. That was the moment I understood we were forming a long convoy and that there were many girl soldiers. Well, when I call them "soldiers" . . . let's just say they looked like soldiers, though most of them had neither stripes nor weapons. Perhaps, I told myself, they are no more soldiers than I am. In any case, I was the youngest, which made some of them smile when they turned around to take a look at me. I'd just turned fifteen, but later on I'd run into girls who were only twelve.

In Sirte the convoy vanished inside the Katiba al-Saadi, the military compound named for one of Gaddafi's sons. They quickly assigned rooms to us and I found out that I was to share mine with Farida, one of Gaddafi's bodyguards, a girl who was twenty-three or twenty-four years old. Salma put a suitcase on my bed. "Be quick about it! Go take a shower!" she yelled as she clapped her hands. "And put on the blue nightgown!" As soon as she was gone I looked at Farida.

"What's all this madness? Would you please explain to me what I'm doing here?"

"I can't tell you anything. I'm a soldier. I follow orders. Just do the same."

The discussion was closed. I watched her fastidiously organize her things, unable to decide to do anything, especially not to put on the clothes I found in the suitcase—a tangle of G-strings, bras, and baby-dolls, plus a robe. But Salma came back. "I told you to get ready! Your master is waiting!" She stayed there until I'd put on the blue negligee and then had me follow her upstairs. She made me wait in a hallway. Mabrouka arrived, with a sour look on her face, and pushed me into a bedroom, closing the door behind me.

He was naked. Lying on a large bed with beige sheets in a windowless room of the same color, he seemed to be buried in sand. The blue of my nightie presented a contrast. "Come here, my little whore!" he said as he opened his arms. "Come on, don't be afraid!" Afraid? I was far beyond any fear. I was going to the slaughterhouse. I was dreaming of some way to escape but knew that Mabrouka was lying in ambush behind the door. I remained motionless, so he leaped to his feet and with a force that took me by surprise he grabbed my arm, threw me on the bed, and flung himself on top of me. I tried to push him away, but he was heavy and I couldn't manage it. He bit my neck, my cheeks, my chest. I fought back, screaming. He shouted, "Don't move, you dirty whore!" He beat me, crushed my breasts, and then after pulling up my dress and pinning my arms down, he brutally penetrated me.

I will never forget that moment. He violated my body, but he pierced my soul with a dagger. The blade never came out.

I was devastated. I had no strength left and I stayed completely still, just weeping. He rose to get a small red towel he kept within arm's reach, ran it between my thighs, and disappeared into the bathroom. Much later I found out that this blood was important to him for some black magic ceremony.

I bled for three days. Galina came to my bedside to attend to my injuries; she caressed my forehead, saying that I was injured inside. I didn't complain. I no longer asked any questions.

"How can anyone do that to a child? It's horrible!" she'd said to Mabrouka, who'd delivered me to her. But Mabrouka didn't care. I hardly touched the food they brought to my room. I was like a dead person walking. Farida ignored me.

On the fourth day Salma came to get me: the master had asked for me. Mabrouka took me into his room. And he started all over again, with the same violence and using the same awful words. I bled profusely, and Galina warned Mabrouka: "Don't let them touch her again! Next time it will be really dangerous."

On the fifth day they brought me to his room at dawn. He was having his breakfast: garlic cloves and watermelon juice, cookies dunked in tea with camel's milk. He put a cassette of ancient Bedouin songs into an old tape recorder and shouted at me: "Go on, dance, you whore! Dance!" I hesitated. "Go on, go on!" He was clapping his hands. I started a small movement and then continued tentatively. The sound was awful, the songs outdated, and he was staring at me lecherously. Women were coming in to clear his dishes or whisper something to him, indifferent to my presence. "Keep going, you slut!" he said without taking his eyes off me. His penis grew hard; he got up to grab me, slapped me on the thighs. "What a whore!" And then he sprawled all over me. That same evening he forced me to smoke a cigarette. He said that he liked the way women looked when inhaling smoke. I didn't want to. He lit one and put it in my mouth. "Breathe in! Swallow the smoke! Swallow it!" I was coughing, which made him laugh. "Go on! Another one!"

On the sixth day he received me with a whiskey in his hand. "It's time you started drinking, my whore!" It was Black Label, a bottle with a characteristic black mark that I would recognize anywhere. I'd always heard that the Koran forbade the drinking of alcohol and that Gaddafi was an extremely religious man. At school and on television they presented him as the finest defender of Islam, always referring to the Koran, leading prayers amid the crowds. So to see him drink whiskey like that was completely unbelievable. You have no idea what a shock it was. The man presented as the father of the Libyans, as the builder of the law, of justice, and as the guardian of absolute authority was violating all the beliefs he professed! Everything was a sham. Everything my teachers taught us, everything in which my parents believed was a lie. "If they only knew!" I said to myself. He handed me a glass. "Drink, you whore!" I wet my lips, felt something burn and despised the taste. "Come on, drink it! Like medicine!"

That same night we all left, in convoy, for Tripoli: a dozen cars or so, the huge camper van, and a pickup loaded with equipment, including a lot of large tents. All the girls were in uniform again and all of them looked thrilled to be leaving. I was in despair. Leaving Sirte meant I'd be even farther away from my parents, losing any chance to go back home. I tried to imagine a way to escape, but it was useless. Was there a single place in Libya where one could escape Gaddafi? His police, his militia, his spies were everywhere. Neighbors kept an eye on neighbors and even within some families there might be denunciations. I was his prisoner and at his mercy. The girl sitting next to me in the car noticed my tears. "Oh, little one! They told me they took you from school . . ." I didn't answer. Through the window I was watching Sirte vanish in the distance. I was unable to say a word. "Oh, it will be all right!" the girl next to the driver called out. "We're all in the same situation."

3

BAB AL-AZIZIA

"Ah! Tripoli at last!" My neighbor looked so delighted to see the first houses of the city that I began to feel somewhat reassured. "I'm sick of Sirte!" the other girl added. I didn't know what to make of their comments but I was taking it all in, focused and eager to catch the least bit of information. We'd been driving for close to four hours at very high speed, startling other cars and passersby, who would move aside to let the convoy pass. Night had now fallen and from afar the city was a jumble of streets, towers, and lights.

Suddenly we slowed down to go through the vast gate of a huge fortified compound. Soldiers stood at attention, but the relaxed attitude of the girls in the car implied that they felt they were coming home. One of them simply told me: "This is Bab al-Azizia."

Of course, I was familiar with the name. Who in Libya wasn't? It was the place of power above all others, the center of authority and omnipotence: the fortified residence of Colonel Gaddafi. In Arabic the name means "The Gate of Azizia," the region that extends to the west of Tripoli; but in the minds of Libyans it is above all a symbol of terror. Once, Papa had taken me to see the enormous gate, crowned with a gargantuan poster of the Guide, as well as the surrounding wall, which was several kilometers long. It wouldn't have entered anyone's head to walk the full length of the wall, which would have been an invitation to be arrested for espionage or even shot at. We'd actually been told that an unlucky cabdriver, who unfortunately had had a flat tire at the foot of the wall, died when his car was blown up even before he could take his spare out of the trunk. And cell phones weren't allowed anywhere in the surrounding district.

We'd come through the main gate, entering an area that seemed immense to me. Rows of stark buildings with narrow openings, really just slits, for windows, which had to be soldiers' quarters. Lawns, palm trees, gardens, dromedaries, austere buildings, and a few villas tucked away in the greenery. Other than the countless security doors we passed through one after another and a succession of walls whose configuration I didn't understand, the place didn't seem too hostile to me. Finally, the car parked in front of a large house. Mabrouka immediately appeared, acting like the mistress of the house. "Come in! And put your things in your room." I followed the other girls, who walked through an entrance made of cement and shaped like a gentle slope, then climbed down a few steps and came to a porch with a metal detector. The air was cool and very humid. In fact, we were in the basement. Amal, my neighbor in the car, pointed to a small window-less room: "This room will be yours." I pushed open the door. The walls were adorned with mirrors, which meant it was impossible to get away from your reflection. Two narrow beds were pushed into corners on either side of the room, which also had a table, a television, and a small adjoining bathroom. I got undressed, took a shower, and lay down to sleep. But it was impossible. I turned on the TV and wept quietly, listening to Egyptian songs.

In the middle of the night Amal came into the room. "Quick, put on a pretty negligee! We're going up to see the Guide together." Amal was a true beauty. Wearing shorts and a little satin tank top, she really looked lovely; I myself was very impressed. I put on the red nightie she pointed at, we climbed a little staircase just to the right of my room that I hadn't noticed before, and we found ourselves in front of the master's bedroom, directly above mine. It was a huge room, partly sur-rounded by mirrors, with a large four-poster bed framed in red netting like that of the sultans in *A Thousand and One Nights,* a round table, some shelves with a few books and DVDs, a col-lection of small bottles of oriental perfume with which Gad-dafi often dabbed his neck, and a desk with a large computer. Facing the bed was a sliding door that went into a bathroom with a big Jacuzzi. Oh, I forgot—near the desk was a small corner reserved for prayer, with a few intensely ornate and valuable copies of the Koran. I mention it because it intrigued me; I never saw Gaddafi pray. Never. Except for the one time in Africa when he himself had to deliver an important public prayer. When I think about it: what a show he put on!

When we entered his room he was sitting on his bed in a red jogging suit. "Ah!" he roared. "Come and dance for me, my little whores! Come on, let's go, let's go!" He put the same old cassette in a tape recorder and, swaying a little, snapped his fingers. "You have such piercing eyes, they could kill . . ." How many times did I hear that ridiculous song! He couldn't get enough of it. Amal was doing her best, fully participating in his game, winking at him, and acting terribly coy. I couldn't get over it. She was gyrating, shaking her bottom, her breasts, closing her eyes as she slowly lifted her hair, only to let it fall again and then turn around with her head back. I continued to be on my guard, supple as a piece of wood, my eyes hostile. Then she started to move toward me to include me in her dance, brushing against my hip, sliding her thigh between my legs, and encouraging me to move with her. "Oh, yes, my little whores!" the Guide cried out.

He got undressed, motioned to me to keep dancing, and called Amal over to him. She moved toward him and began to suck his penis. I didn't believe what I was seeing and asked, with hope in my voice: "Shall I leave now?"

"No, you come here, you slut!"

He pulled me by my hair, forced me to sit down, and kissed me—or, really, nibbled on my face while Amal kept doing what she was doing. Then, still holding me tightly by my hair, he said: "Watch and learn from her. You'll have to do the same thing." He thanked Amal and asked her to shut the door behind her. Then he threw himself on me and kept at it for a long time. Mabrouka was coming and going as if nothing was happening. She was giving him messages—"Leila Trabelsi wants you to call her back"—until she finally said: "Stop now. You have other things to do." I was stunned. She could say anything to him; I actually think he was afraid of her. He went into the bathroom, into the Jacuzzi, which she had filled with water, and yelled at me: "Hand me a towel." They were within arm's reach of him but he wanted me to serve him. "Perfume my back." Then he pointed at a bell near the tape recorder, which I rang. And Mabrouka was inside in a flash. "Give this little slut some DVDs so she can learn her job."

Salma showed up in my room five minutes later with a DVD player she'd taken from another inmate and a pile of DVDs. "Here, here's some porn. Watch it carefully and learn! The master will be furious if you're not up to snuff. This is your homework!"

My God, school . . . That was already so far away. I took a shower. Although she had her own room, Amal settled down on the other bed. It had been a week since I'd spoken with anyone and I was beside myself with anxiety and loneliness.

"Amal, I don't know what I'm doing here. This is not my life, this isn't normal. I miss Mama every moment of the day. Can't I phone her, at least?"

"I'll speak to Mabrouka about it."

Exhausted, I fell asleep.

There was a knock on my door and Salma unexpectedly came in. "Go upstairs, just as you are. Quickly! Your master wants to see you." It was eight o'clock in the morning and I'd only slept for a few hours. Clearly, Gaddafi himself had just woken up, too. He was still in bed, his hair disheveled, and was stretching. "Come into my bed, you whore!" Salma pushed me viciously. "And you, bring us our breakfast in bed." He ripped off my sweat suit and jumped on me in a fury. "Did you watch the films, slut? Now you ought to know what to do!" He was growling and biting me all over. He raped me again. And then afterward he got up to eat a garlic clove, a habit which caused him to have perpetually foul breath. "Now get out of here, you slut." As I left the room, Galina and two other Ukrainian nurses went in. That was the morning I really understood I was dealing with a madman.

But who knew it? Papa, Mama, the Libyans . . . No one knew what was going on at Bab al-Azizia. Everyone was scared stiff of Gaddafi, because resisting or criticizing him meant being thrown into prison or put to death, and because he truly was terrifying even when you called him Papa Muammar and sang the anthem in front of his photograph. Going from there to imagining what he'd done to me . . . It was so humiliating, so offensive, so incredible. That was it: it was incredible! So I knew nobody would believe me! I would never be able to tell my story, because it was Muammar. So, in addition to having been defiled by him, I was the one people would consider mad.

I was thinking about all of this when Amal stuck her head inside my door: "Come, don't just stay here, let's walk around!" We went through the hallway, climbed up four steps, and found ourselves inside a large well-equipped kitchen with a poster on one wall of a dark-haired young girl, a bit older than I, whom Amal identified for me as Hana Gaddafi, the Colonel's adopted daughter. It wasn't until much later that I learned her death had been mistakenly announced in 1986, following the American bombing of Tripoli that Reagan ordered. But it was no secret to anyone at Bab al-Azizia that she was not only alive but the Guide's favorite child. Amal made coffee and took out a small cell phone. My eyes opened wide. "How come you're allowed to have a telephone?"

"Sweetie! Let me remind you that I've been inside these walls for more than ten years!"

The kitchen continued into a kind of cafeteria that gradually filled with very beautiful young girls, all heavily made-up and accompanied by two boys wearing the badge of the Department of Protocol. There was lots of squealing and laughing.

"Who are they?" I asked Amal.

"Guests of Muammar. He has them constantly. But please, be discreet, and don't ask any more questions!"

I saw the Ukrainian nurses, in white jackets or turquoise vests, going back and forth and told myself that, apparently, every guest was made to have a blood test. Since Amal had vanished, I went back to my room. What would I say to those girls who looked so thrilled with the prospect of meeting the Guide? Ask them to help me get out of here? Before I could explain my story I would be cornered and thrown into some hole.

I was lying on my bed when Mabrouka pushed the door open (I was forbidden to close it completely). "Watch the DVDs we gave you—that's an order!" I put in a disc without having the slightest idea of what I was about to watch. It was the first time I had ever seen anything having to do with sex. I was in unfamiliar territory, both at a loss and completely sickened. After turning off the DVD, I soon fell asleep, and then Amal woke me up to take me to the kitchen for lunch.

It's unbelievable how bad the food was at the home of the president of Libya! The meals were served on cheap white metal dishes, and the food itself was disgusting. My disbelief made Amal smile; then, as we were leaving, she suggested I come and see her room. And that's where Mabrouka surprised us. She shouted: "Both of you, back to your own room! You know very well, Amal, you're not allowed to visit each other! Don't ever do that again!"

In the middle of the night Mabrouka came to get me: "Your master is asking for you." She opened his door and threw me at him. He made me dance. Then smoke. Then he placed some very fine white powder on a business card. He produced some thin paper, rolled it into a cone, and snorted it. "Go on, do what I'm doing! Snort it, you whore! Snort it! You'll see the result!"

The cocaine irritated my throat, my nose, my eyes. I coughed and felt sick to my stomach. "That's because you didn't take enough!" he told me. He moistened a cigarette with his saliva, rolled it in the cocaine powder, and smoked it slowly, forcing me to have some puffs and swallow the smoke. I didn't feel well. I was conscious but very weak. "Now dance!" he ordered.

My head was spinning, I didn't know where I was; everything was getting hazy, foggy. He got up and clapped his hands to the beat and put the cigarette back in my mouth. I collapsed, and he raped me savagely. Over and over again. He was excited and violent. At one point he suddenly stopped, put on a pair of glasses, and picked up a book for a few minutes, then came back to me, biting, crushing my breasts, taking me again before going to his computer to check his e-mail or say a word or two to Mabrouka, only to attack me once more. I bled again. Around five in the morning he said: "Get out!" And I went back to my room to cry.

Late in the morning Amal came to suggest we have lunch. I didn't want to leave my room, didn't want to see anyone, but she insisted, so we ate in the cafeteria. It was Friday, the day of prayer. They served us couscous. Then I saw a group of young men arrive, smiling and very much at ease. "Is that the new one?" they asked Amal when they noticed me. She nodded and they introduced themselves, quite courteously: Jalal, Faisal, Abdelhaïm, Ali, Adnane, Houssam. Then they headed for the Guide's bedroom.

That was the day I had the second great shock of my life, and from that moment on my expression would never be pure again. I'm not telling you this with any joy. I'm forcing myself because I committed myself to telling my story, as a testimony, and because people need to understand why this monster enjoyed such complete impunity. But the scenes are so cruel and humiliating to describe, so embarrassing and shameful for me and the other bystanders whom Gaddafi insidiously turned into accomplices so that they would never risk recounting his perversions. This was a man who had seized the power to decide over the life and death of others, a man who defiled all those who had the misfortune of coming near him.

Mabrouka called me. "Get dressed, your master wants you," which meant: "Get undressed and go upstairs." She pushed the door open, and then an insane scene appeared before my eyes. The Guide was naked, sodomizing Ali, while Houssam was dancing, dressed and made up like a woman, to that same languid Egyptian song. I wanted to run back to my room but Houssam cried out "Master, there's Soraya!" and motioned me to dance with him. I was paralyzed. Then Gaddafi called out:

53

"Come here, slut." He threw Ali aside and seized me furiously. Houssam was dancing, Ali was watching, and, for the second time in a few days, I wanted to die. They had no right to do this to me.

And then Mabrouka came in and ordered the boys to leave and the master to stop because there was an emergency. He withdrew immediately and told me to get the hell out. I ran to my room, sobbing, and stayed in the shower for the rest of the evening. I kept washing myself and crying. I simply couldn't stop. He was insane, they were all insane; it was a house of lunatics, and I didn't want to be among them a moment longer. I wanted my parents, my brothers, my sister; I wanted my old life. But that was no longer possible. He had wrecked everything. He was repulsive. And he was the president of my country.

Amal came to see me and I begged her: "Please, please speak to Mabrouka. I can't take this anymore, I want my mother . . ." I saw her become emotional for the first time. "Oh, my little darling!" she said, taking me in her arms. "Your story is so much like mine. They took me from school as well. I was fourteen." She was now twenty-five and loathed her life.

4

RAMADAN

One day I found out that Gaddafi and his coterie were supposed to leave on an official visit to Dakar and that I wouldn't be traveling with them. What a relief. For three days I was able to breathe and move around freely between my room and the cafeteria, where I'd see Amal and a few other girls, including Fatiha, who had stayed behind on guard duty at Bab al-Azizia. They smoked, drank coffee, and chatted. I kept quiet, on the lookout for the tiniest bit of information on how this deranged community functioned. Sadly, they never said anything of substance. However, I did find out that Amal was able to go out during the day with a driver from Bab al-Azizia, which completely astonished me. She was free . . . and she came back? How in the world did that make sense? Why didn't she run away, as I'd dreamed of doing every second I'd been inside these walls? There were so many things I simply didn't understand.

I also discovered that most of the girls, known as "revolutionary guards," were given a card, which I thought was a badge but which was an actual identity card. It had their picture, their first name, and the title "Daughter of Muammar Gaddafi" in bold letters above the personal signature and a small photo of the Guide. This "daughter" title seemed rather overblown to me. But the card itself was clearly an open door to the area just outside the compound of Bab al-Azizia and even to the city itself, after one went through countless security doors that were guarded by armed soldiers. Much later on, I heard that the status of these "daughters" and the true nature of their function did not fool anyone. But they valued their card. Sure, they were seen as whores, but still, they were whores of the supreme Guide, and that earned them respect anywhere they went.

The group returned on the fourth day and the whole of the basement was in a fever of excitement. Along with his baggage, the Guide had brought back a large number of African women, some very young, some older, all heavily made-up, showing off their cleavage, wearing boubous or skintight jeans. Mabrouka was playing mistress of the house and fussing over them. "Amal! Soraya! Hurry, bring coffee and cake!" So we had to dash between the kitchen and the drawing rooms, zigzagging between the cheerful women, all eager to see the Colonel. He was still in his office, meeting with some important-looking

African gentlemen. But when they left I saw the women go up, one after another, to the Guide's bedroom. I was watching them from afar, dying to tell them, "Watch out, he's a monster!" but also: "Help me get out of here!" Mabrouka caught my gaze and seemed annoyed that we'd stayed in the room when she'd asked Faisal to serve. "Each of you to your own room," she commanded, clapping her hands.

Salma came to get me in the middle of the night and brought me to Gaddafi's door. He made me smoke one cigarette after another, and then he . . . What word should I use? It was so degrading. I was now no more than an object, a hole. I clenched my teeth, dreading his blows. Then he put on a cassette of the Tunisian singer Nawal Ghachem, and demanded that I dance, over and over and over again, completely naked this time. Salma came in, whispered a few words to him, and straightaway he told me: "You can leave, my love." What had come over him? He'd never addressed me with anything but insults.

A low-ranking policewoman, twenty-three years old, ended up in my room the next day. "This is Najah," Mabrouka said. "She's going to spend two days with you." The girl seemed nice enough—direct, and just a tad brazen. And she really wanted to talk. "They're all just bastards, you know!" she began the first evening. "They never keep a promise. I've been with them for seven years and still I've never been compensated! Received nothing! Not a thing. Not even a house!" "Watch out," I said to myself. "Don't get involved—she may want to set a trap for me." But she continued confiding in me, and I let her.

"I heard you were the new young one. Are you getting used to life at Bab al-Azizia?"

"You have no idea how much I miss my mother."

"That will pass . . ."

"If only I could get in touch with her!"

"She'll find out soon enough what you're doing."

"Do you have any advice how I could contact her?"

"If there's any advice I would give you, it's to get out of here!"

"But I'm a prisoner! I have no choice!"

"Me, I stay two days, sleep with Gaddafi, which gets me a little money, and I go home."

"But I don't want that either! That's not my kind of life."

"You want to get out? Well, play at being a troublemaker! Put up a fight, make noise, create some problems."

"But they'll kill me! I know they're more than capable of that. When I resisted he beat me up and raped me."

"Tell yourself that he likes hardheaded girls."

Then she lay down on her bed, eating pistachio nuts, and watched a porno flick. "You should always be learning!" she said, urging me to watch with her. I was dumbfounded. Learn? After she'd just recommended that I put up a fight? I'd rather sleep.

The next night we were both called to the Guide's bedroom. Najah was all excited over the prospect of seeing him again. "Why don't you put on a black nightie," she suggested before we went up. When the door opened he was naked, and Najah threw herself at him: "My love! How I've missed you!" He looked pleased. "So come here, you whore!" Then turning to me, hopping mad: "Why are you wearing that color I so abhor? Get out of here! Go change!" I rushed down the stairs, noticed Amal in her room, and bummed a cigarette from her. And smoked it once I was back in my room. It was the first time I'd ever lit one on my own, the first time I'd felt the need to smoke. But Salma didn't let me: "What in the hell are you doing? Your master is waiting for you!" She took me back into his room at the very moment Najah was painstakingly replaying the scenes from the video. "Put the cassette on and dance!" Gaddafi ordered me. But then he leaped off the bed, ripped off my nightie, and violently raped me. "Get out!" he then said, dismissing me with a motion of his hand. I left the room, badly bruised.

When Najah, too, returned, I asked her why she had suggested I wear a color he hated. "It's very strange," she answered without even looking at me. "Usually he likes black. Perhaps it doesn't suit you very well . . . But in the end isn't that just what you wanted? Something to divert his attention away from you?" It suddenly occurred to me that there might be some rivalry between Gaddafi's girls. What an insane idea! They could keep him for all I cared!

I woke up the next morning wanting a cigarette. I found Amal having coffee with another girl and asked her for one.

She picked up her phone and placed an order: "Would you get some Marlboro Lights and some Slims for us, please?" I couldn't believe how simple it was! Indeed, all you needed to do was call a driver, who'd stock up and bring the supplies to the garage, where an employee of the house would get them. "It's not good for you at your age," Amal said to me. "Don't fall into the cigarette trap."

"But you smoke, too! And we have the same life."

She gave me a long look and a sad smile.

Ramadan was approaching, and one morning I heard that the entire household was moving to Sirte. They gave me a uniform again, told me which car in the convoy I would ride in, and within a few moments I felt the sun caress my face. It had been weeks since I'd left the basement and I was happy to see a little sky. When we arrived at the military compound, the Katiba al-Saadi, Mabrouka came to me and said: "You wanted to see your mother. Well, you're going to see her." My heart stopped. I'd been thinking about her every second since my abduction. I dreamed of disappearing in her arms. Day and night I imagined what I would say to her, stumbling over my words, then picking up the story, and trying to reassure myself that she'd understand without my providing any details. Oh, my God! What I wouldn't have given to see my parents again, my brothers, my little sister Noura . . .

The car parked across the street from our white building. The original trio—Mabrouka, Salma, and Faiza—accompanied me to the entrance, and I rushed into the stairwell. Mama was waiting for me in our apartment on the third floor. The little ones were at school. We both wept and embraced each other very tightly. She held me close to kiss me, looked me in the eye, laughed, shook her head, wiped away her tears. "Oh, Soraya! You broke my heart! Talk to me, say something!" I couldn't. I shook my head, hugging her chest. Then she said softly: "Faiza explained to me that Gaddafi took your virginity. My little girl, my little girl! You're much too young to become a woman . . ." Faiza was coming up the stairs. I heard her loud voice: "That's enough! Come on down!" Mama clung to me. "Leave my child here with me!" The other woman was already there, looking stern. "God help us," Mama said. "What can I tell your brothers? Everyone is wondering where you are and I answer that you've gone to Tunisia to visit the family or to Tripoli with your father. I'm telling lies to everybody. What are we going to do, Soraya? What will become of you?" Faiza tore me away from her. "When will you bring her back to me again?" Mama asked in tears. "Someday!" And we went back to the Katiba.

Fatiha was waiting for me. "Your master is asking for you." When I came into that sand-colored room of his where he'd raped me weeks earlier, Galina and four other Ukrainian women were with him. Galina was massaging Gaddafi while the others sat around him. I waited by the door, strapped in my uniform, still totally overcome by my visit with Mama. How he disgusted me, this monster who thought he was God, stank of garlic and sweat, and thought of nothing but fucking. Once the nurses left, he commanded: "Get undressed!" I wanted to shout "You poor bastard!" and then leave, slamming the door behind me, but in despair I did what he told me. "Get on top of me! You've been learning your lessons, haven't you? And stop eating. You've gained weight—I don't like that!" When it was over he did something he'd never done before. He dragged me over to the Jacuzzi, made me climb up onto the edge of the shower, and urinated on me.

I shared my room with Farida, the same girl who was there during my first stay at the Katiba. She was lying down, feeling sick, and she was very pale. "I have hepatitis," she told me.

"Hepatitis? But I thought the Guide had a phobia about illnesses."

"Yes, but it seems that this one is not sexually transmitted."

How was it transmitted then? I started to be afraid. That very evening Gaddafi called for us both. He was naked, impatient, and told Farida straightaway: "Come here, slut." I took advantage of the opportunity: "So I can go?" He had the expression of a madman: "Dance!" I said to myself: "He's fucking a woman with hepatitis and I'm going to be next." And so I was, while Farida was told to take her turn dancing.

We stayed in Sirte for three days. He called for me numerous times. Sometimes there were two, three, four girls at the same time. We didn't talk to each other. Each girl had her own story, her own fate. And her own saga of misfortune.

* * *

Finally it was Ramadan. For my family this was a sacred period, and my mother was very strict about it. There was no question of eating between sunrise and sunset, you'd say the appropriate prayers, and at night you'd feast on delicious things. That's what I decided to think about all day long before I finally got back to my family. Occasionally, Mama even took us to Morocco and Tunisia to share this time with my grandmother and great-grandmother. It was really marvelous. From the age of two I'd never failed to observe Ramadan, nor even imagined that its rules could be violated. And yet, the night before the beginning of Ramadan, when you are supposed to prepare yourself spiritually to enter into this special period, to silence all desires and senses, Gaddafi tried to hunt me down. The pursuit went on for hours and I felt completely helpless. "This is forbidden, it's Ramadan!" I pleaded with him at dawn. Other than his commands and insults, he never said a word to me. This time, however, he deigned to answer between two growls: "The only thing that's forbidden is eating." To me, that was blasphemy.

And so I learned how Gaddafi had no respect for anything at all. Not even for Allah! He violated every one of his commandments. He defied even God! Bewildered, I went back down to my room. I had to talk to someone very soon—Amal or another one of the girls. I was truly in shock. But I found no one. I was barred from wandering through the hallways and the basement labyrinth, which was lit by neon lights. My perimeters were extremely limited: my room, his room, the kitchen, the cafeteria, plus on occasion the reception rooms near his office and his small private exercise room. That was it.

I heard footsteps and the sound of doors opening and closing above my head and knew that Amal and other girls were rushing into the Guide's bedroom. On Ramadan! When I saw them at dinner that evening I told them how utterly appalled I was. What they were doing was a crime against God, wasn't it? They burst out laughing! As long as he didn't come, he had explained to them, as long as he didn't ejaculate it didn't count in the eyes of Allah. My eyes opened wide, and that made them laugh even harder. "It's Ramadan Gaddafi style," one of the girls concluded.

He made me come upstairs throughout the month of Ramadan, no matter what hour of the day or night. He'd smoke, he'd fuck, he'd beat me as he howled. And gradually I allowed myself to eat no matter what time of the day it was. What was the use of respecting rules in a universe that had no limits, no law, no logic. I even ended up wondering why my mother made such a fuss over observing any of the Ramadan rituals.

The twenty-seventh night of Ramadan is known as the Night of Destiny and commemorates the revelation of the Koran to the Prophet. It is often the occasion for grand night-time festivities and I learned that, indeed, Gaddafi was going to receive a large number of prestigious guests in his reception halls and an adjacent tent. Mabrouka called us all together so we could put cakes and fruit on platters and serve. I was wearing a black jogging suit with a red sash on the side and I remember that my hair, which came down to my waist, wasn't held together by a headband or in a bun, as I sometimes wore it. The guests arrived all at the same time and the three halls filled up. There were many spectacularly beautiful African women. Men wearing ties, military men.

Unfortunately, I recognized nobody—with one exception! Nuri Mesmari, the chief of protocol, with his hair and strange blond beard, his one glass eye behind elegant glasses. I'd seen him on television, and it was strange to see him here, flitting about among the guests. Another man arrived, Saada Al Fallah, who seemed to know the girls personally and handed each one an envelope with five hundred dinars. Pocket money, they told me. I caught his glance several times and sensed he had noticed me. He came over to me, smiling. "Ah! So this is the new little one! Really, how lovely she is!" He laughed as he pinched my cheek, half flirtatious, half paternal. The scene didn't escape Mabrouka, who promptly called him over: "Saada, come to me right now!" Amal, who was standing close to me, whispered in my ear: "She saw it! Go back to your room quickly. This is serious, I can assure you."

So I rushed off, a little worried. An hour or two later Mabrouka pushed open my door. "Go upstairs!" I presented myself at the Guide's bedroom with Mabrouka on my heels. He was in the process of slipping into a brick red jogging suit and stared at me with a hateful look. "Come here, slut . . . So, you're playing with your hair to lead everyone on? To be expected, of course: your mother is Tunisian!"

"I promise you, Master, I've done nothing wrong."

"You've done nothing wrong, slut? You have the gall to say you did nothing wrong?"

"Nothing! What could I have done?"

"Something you'll not be doing again, you whore!"

Whereupon, yanking me by the hair, he forced me down on my knees and ordered Mabrouka: "Give me a knife!" I thought he was going to kill me. His eyes were wild; I knew he was ready for anything. Mabrouka handed him a knife. He snatched it and, still holding my hair in his iron fist, cut furiously into the mass with great sharp slashes and terrifying yowling. "You thought you could play around with that, did you? Well, that's done with!" Chunks of black hair were falling down beside me. He kept on going—cutting, slicing. Then he turned around abruptly. "Finish this!" he yelled at Mabrouka.

I was sobbing, traumatized, incapable of keeping my body from shaking. With each slash of the knife I felt he was about to slit my throat or split my skull. I was on the ground like an animal that he might slaughter. Parts of my hair still touched my shoulders, but I could tell Gaddafi had cut others, since I couldn't feel any hair brushing my neck anymore. It was complete butchery. "You look terrible!" Farida exclaimed when she passed me a little while later, not caring to know the reason why. I didn't see the Guide for several days thereafter. But I did see his wife.

The occasion was the feast of Eid, the day that Ramadan fasting officially comes to an end. Usually it is a warm family celebration, with morning prayers, a short trip to the mosque, and then a visit to family and friends. When I was a little girl I loved that day. But what was I to expect, or rather fear, from this day at Bab al-Azizia? I didn't have a clue. In the morning Mabrouka brought us together: "Quickly, get dressed properly. And behave yourselves! The Guide's wife is coming here." Safia? The wife? In the past I had seen her photograph but since my abduction I had never yet run across her. I had heard them say that she had her own house somewhere within Bab al-Azizia but that Gaddafi never slept there and that they got together only very rarely, usually at public events. The Guide, the "enemy of polygamy," was living with countless women but not with his own wife, although some people did say that he would meet his daughters every Friday in El-Morabaat, his villa on the road to the airport. Thus the announcement created a bit of a shock: Gaddafi's sexual slaves had to be dressed up as domestic servants and maids! So when, after a multitude of other visitors, Safia entered the house with an imposing, haughty look and headed for the Guide's bedroom, I was in the kitchen with the other girls, busily doing dishes, cleaning the stove, and scrubbing the floor. Cinderella. She had barely left when Mabrouka announced for all to hear: "Everything back to normal!"

Indeed. The master called for me immediately. "Dance!" He summoned Adnane, a former member of the special guard, who was married (to one of Gaddafi's quasi-official mistresses) and the father of two children. He frequently forced Adnane to have sexual relations with him. He sodomized him in front of me and screamed: "Your turn, you whore!"

5

HAREM

He was flying to Chad for six days, with Mabrouka, Salma, Faiza, and a great many girls among his luggage. Perhaps this was an opportunity for me to see Mama, I said to myself. I tried my luck with Mabrouka, begging her to let me visit my mother during their absence. "Out of the question!" she answered. "You'll stay in your room and be ready to join us at any moment in case your master asks for you. I'll send an airplane for you." An airplane . . .

So I gave my body a rest. A body that was perpetually covered with bruises and bites that wouldn't heal. A worn-out body made up of nothing but pain, a body that I didn't like. I smoked, snacked, dozed, lay on my bed watching videos on the little television in my room. I remember not thinking about anything at all. The evening before their return, though, I had a nice surprise: one of the Bab al-Azizia drivers had been given permission to take me out for half an hour, enough time to spend the five hundred dinars we each received for Ramadan. It was unheard of. I saw again the sweetness of springtime; I was dazzled by the light, like a blind woman discovering the sun. My windowless basement was so humid that Mabrouka always burned herbs there to chase away the smell of mildew.

The driver took me to an elegant area, where I bought a jogging outfit, shoes, and a shirt. I didn't know what to get. I'd never had any money of my own and was totally confused. Besides, why should I dress up? Between the Guide's room and mine I basically needed almost nothing. How stupid of me, now that I think of it! I should have thought of getting a book, something that would make me dream, escape, or learn about life. Or else a notebook and a pencil, to draw or write, for I had no access to anything of the sort at Bab al-Azizia. Only Amal had a few books in her room—romance novels and a book on Marilyn Monroe I dreamed of but that she refused to lend to me. But no, I didn't think of anything intelligent or useful like that. I just looked around greedily and confused. My blood was bubbling. I felt dizzy. I was a prisoner, let out for a few minutes in a city that knew nothing about me, where the passersby on the sidewalk couldn't begin to guess my story, where the salesman handed me my package with a smile as if I were a normal customer, where a small group of high school girls in uniform chatted noisily next to me without thinking that I, too, should have been in school, my only preoccupations studying and having fun. For once I didn't have Mabrouka on my back, but, although the driver was nice, I felt like I was being stalked. Fleeing was not an option. My thirty minutes of pseudo-freedom seemed like thirty seconds to me.

The next morning the group was back. I heard a racket coming up from the basement—footsteps, doors opening and closing, loud voices. I was careful not to leave my room but Mabrouka soon appeared in the doorway and commanded "Upstairs!" with a motion of her chin. She didn't even say "You have to go upstairs" anymore. A minimum of words. A maximum of scorn. Yes, I was treated as a slave. And that ghastly order to go to the master's room triggered an electric wave of anxiety throughout my body.

"Ah, my love! Come here!" he said when he saw me. Then he pounced on me, yelling "whore" and growling. I was just a puppet he could manipulate and abuse. I was no longer human to him. Fatiha interrupted him as she entered: "Master, you are needed, it's urgent." He pushed me away, hissing between clenched teeth "Let go!" and I went back down to my humid little room. For the first time that day I watched a porn video, wondering about sex. The little I knew about it was nothing but violence, horror, domination, cruelty, and sadism. It was a torture session, and always with the same assailant. I couldn't even imagine it might be otherwise. But the actresses in the video weren't playing the roles of slaves or victims. They were even developing ways to have sex they seemed to appreciate as much as their partners did. It was odd and intriguing.

Two days later Faiza came into my room with a piece of paper. "Here is your mother's number, you may call her from the office." Mama immediately picked up: "Oh, Soraya! How is my little girl? Oh, my God, I'm so happy to hear your voice! Where are you? When can I see you? Are you healthy?" I was allowed only one minute. Just like all prisoners. Faiza said: "That's enough." And with one finger she disconnected us.

Then one day a strange thing happened. Najah, the fearless policewoman I had met when I first arrived at Bab al-Azizia, came to spend two days there, as she did from time to time. Again she shared my room. I was always a bit wary of her confidences and her cunning, but her gumption entertained me. "I have a plan to let you get some air outside Bab al-Azizia," she told me. "I have the feeling that it would do you good."

"Are you kidding?"

"Not at all. You just have to be clever. Does that appeal to you—a little excursion with me, completely free to do what you want?"

"But they'll never let me go!"

"You're so defeatist! All you have to do is pretend to be sick and I'll take care of the rest."

"That makes no sense! If I really were sick those Ukrainian nurses would take care of me."

"Let me work it out. I'll prepare everything—all you have to do is play along."

* * *

She went to see Mabrouka. I don't know what she told her
but she came back saying we had the green light. It was absolutely incredible. A driver named Amar came to pick us up and
drive us beyond the walls of Bab al-Azizia. I couldn't believe
my eyes. "What is it that you said to Mabrouka?"

"Shhh! First we're going to my place and then I'm taking
you to someone else's house."

"This is crazy! How did you manage that?"

"Hey, my name isn't Najah [success] for nothing!"

"But I have nothing to wear."

"Don't worry. You can use some of my stuff."

We went to her house, changed clothes, and then her sister drove us to a very beautiful villa in Enzara, an area on the
periphery of Tripoli. The owner seemed thrilled to receive
us. "This is the Soraya I told you about," Najah said. The man
looked me over carefully and seemed to be very interested in
me. "So tell me, does that beast hurt you?" I was paralyzed.
Who was this guy? How much could I trust him? I had a horrible premonition and avoided his question. Then Najah's
telephone rang. It was Mabrouka. Najah rolled her eyes and
put the phone back down. "You're not answering?" She didn't
respond, and just handed her glass to the man, who filled it
with whiskey. I was delirious. In this country where the religion as well as the law prohibited the consumption of alcohol,
there were people who allowed themselves to drink without
any shame? And who criticized Gaddafi—who himself was
constantly consuming alcohol? The man handed me a glass,

took offense when I refused, and insisted: "Drink! Go ahead, have a drink! You're free here!"

Najah and her sister didn't have to be asked twice. They started to dance, indicating that the party had begun. They were drinking, laughing, swaying back and forth, their eyes closed. The man watched them eagerly. Another man arrived, sized me up, and smiled. I immediately sensed a trap, but Najah was of no help at all. She was determined to get drunk. I let them know I was tired. Since there was obviously no question of going back, they showed me to a bedroom. I remained on my guard. Very shortly thereafter I heard Najah go up to the adjoining room with the men. The phone kept ringing in the void.

They left me alone, but I woke up with a stone in my stomach. I went to rouse Najah, who was in a complete fog, barely conscious, and remembered nothing of the previous night. Her telephone rang. Mabrouka was shouting: "The driver has been looking for you since yesterday. You'll see what trouble that will get you into with your master!" Najah panicked. She had lied to me, betrayed me, dragged me into a half-baked trap to hand me over to other men like some wild game animal. I was feeling sick. Having been abducted by Gaddafi didn't automatically make me a whore.

Our return to Bab al-Azizia was violent. Mabrouka wasn't there but Salma ordered us both to go upstairs to the Guide. He was foaming with rage. He gave Najah a great slap, bellowing at her: "Now leave. I never want to see you again!"

Then he threw me on the bed and vented all his fury on my body. When he turned around, he muttered between clenched teeth: "All women are whores!" And he added: "Aïsha, too, was a wretched whore!" I believe he was talking about his mother.

A month went by without him touching me. Two new girls from cities in the east had just arrived: a thirteen-year-old from Bayda and a fifteen-year-old from Darnah. I saw them go upstairs to his room, looking innocent, beautiful, and naïve—the way I must have looked a year earlier. I knew exactly what was awaiting them. But I couldn't talk to them or give them the slightest indication. "Did you see the new ones?" Amal asked me. They didn't stay very long. He needed girls every day and usually he'd try them out and discard them or, as I was told, "recycle" them. I didn't know what that meant yet.

The days went by—seasons, national and religious holidays, Ramadans. I was gradually losing any sense of time. Day or night, in the basement the lighting was always the same. And my life was restricted to this narrow field, dependent on the desires and moods of the Colonel. When we'd discuss him among ourselves we gave him no name or title. "He," "Him" were more than enough. He was our center of gravity. There was no possibility of confusion.

I knew nothing about the way the country was going or of the tremors in the rest of the world. Sometimes there were rumors that there was a summit of African leaders or that an eminent head of state was visiting. Most of the meetings took place in the official tent, which "He" would travel to in a golf cart. Before interviews and important discussions, and before all public speeches, he'd smoke hash or take cocaine. He was almost always under the influence of some drug or other. Parties and cocktails were frequently organized in the reception rooms at the house, and attended by the regime's dignitaries and numerous foreign delegations.

We would spot the women right away for, naturally, that's what interested him, and it was Mabrouka's mission to lure them to his room. Students, artists, journalists, models, daughters or wives of prominent or military men, of heads of state. The more prestigious the fathers or husbands were, the more lavish the gifts had to be. A small room next to his office served as Aladdin's cave, where Mabrouka would put the gifts. There I saw Samsonite suitcases filled with wads of dollars and euros, cases with jewelry, gold jewelry sets usually given as wedding gifts, and diamond necklaces. Most of the women had to submit to a blood test, which was administered discreetly by the Ukrainian nurses in a small living room with red seats, located across from the office of the guards. I suppose the wives of state leaders were exempt from this, but I don't know for sure. It always surprised me to see the visiting women head toward his room, immaculately dressed, designer purse in hand, and then come out with their lipstick smudged and their hair undone.

Leila Trabelsi, the wife of the Tunisian dictator Ben Ali, was evidently close to him. She came many times, and Mabrouka adored her. "Oh, Leila my love!" she'd exclaim, always happy to have her on the phone or to announce her arrival. Nothing was too good for her. I specifically recall a box, like a small magic chest, covered in gold. Over time I saw countless wives of African heads of state go to the residence, though I didn't know their names. And Cécilia Sarkozy as well, the wife of the French president—pretty, arrogant—whom the other girls pointed out to me. In Sirte, I saw Tony Blair come out of the Guide's camper. "Hello, girls!" he tossed out to us with an amicable gesture and a cheerful smile.

From Sirte we'd sometimes go to the desert. Gaddafi liked to pitch his tent there, in the middle of nowhere, surrounded by herds of dromedaries. He'd settle down to have tea, talk for hours on end with the elders of his tribe, read, and take naps. He never spent the night; he preferred the comfort of his camper, which is where he'd call for us to join him. In the morning we had to accompany him on the hunt, all of us in uniform. The charade that we were bodyguards was maintained and a woman named Zorah, a true soldier, made sure that I behaved like a professional. One day she was actually given the responsibility of teaching me how to handle a Kalashnikov: take it apart, load it, set it, clean it. "Fire!" she yelled at me when I held the weapon against my shoulder. I refused. I never fired a single shot.

I also discovered the Guide's reliance on black magic, which was Mabrouka's influence. That is how she had a hold over him, they said. She'd consult marabouts and sorcerers all over Africa, and occasionally brought them to the Guide. I saw at least two of them come to the residence: Dr. Salem and Dr. Mohammed Al-Hachemi. He didn't wear any talisman but he put mysterious, always oily ointments on his body, recited incomprehensible formulas, and kept his little red towel close at hand.

Wherever he went, the little crew of Ukrainian nurses—Galina, Elena, Claudia—was always with him. Dressed meticulously in white and blue uniforms, without makeup, they usually worked in the small hospital at Bab al-Azizia but, at his command, could appear at his side in less than five minutes. Not only were they assigned to perform the obligatory blood tests before the Guide's sexual encounters, but they also took care of his personal medical needs and supervised his health and diet. When I expressed worry about getting pregnant I was told that Galina gave the Guide injections that made him infertile. I don't know much about that, but I wasn't confronted with the question of abortion, as were others before me. They all called him Papa, even if he had sexual relations with them; Galina complained about it in front of me. But was there ever a single woman whom he didn't want to possess at least once?

6

AFRICA

Then Jalal, one of the guards at Bab al-Azizia, fell in love with me. Or, at least, he thought he'd fallen in love with me. He'd throw me ardent looks, smile at me as soon as he saw me near the kitchen, and compliment me often. I so much wanted to matter to someone. I didn't know that he was thought to be gay. He let Gaddafi sodomize him, but I was so ignorant that I thought this was just a shocking but perhaps common practice among men. The Guide had very many male sexual partners, including members of the upper ranks of the army.

I needed tenderness, and the thought that a kind, soft-hearted man would show me any affection filled me with a deep warmth. Then he increased the moments of contact, would brush against my hand in passing, whisper that he loved me and even that he dreamed of marrying me someday.

"Didn't you notice that I've been watching you since the day you arrived here?" No, I hadn't noticed, consumed as I was by my misery and loneliness. And besides, any bonds of friendship or support were strictly forbidden in our space.

Jalal grew bold and went to the Guide to declare that he intended to marry me. Gaddafi sent for both of us together. He sniggered, a look of derision on his face. "So you're claiming to be in love, are you? And you have the nerve to tell me about it—me, your master! How would you even dare love someone else, you whore? And you, you pathetic creature, how dare you so much as look at her?" Jalal squirmed. We were both looking at the floor, as pitiful as eight-year-olds. The Guide threw us out. Jalal, though he was a guard, was kept away from the house for two months.

Mabrouka came charging into my room. "You rotten wench! You're thinking of marriage when you haven't even been here three years yet! You're obviously nothing but trash!" Amal, too, came to read me the riot act. "Really, my pet, they're right. You can't be in love with that queer! He's not for you!" Their words only reinforced my attraction to him. Jalal was sweet. And he was the first man to tell me he loved me. What did the scorn of these deranged people matter anyway?

A few months later they announced that the Guide was going to make a grand tour through Africa. Two weeks, five countries, visiting a horde of heads of state. Much was at stake, that was clear; I felt it in Mabrouka's agitation. And the entire household would travel with him. Gaddafi's "daughters," dressed in their lovely uniforms, were to be a special credit to him. Myself included! So, at five o'clock in the morning on June 22, 2007, I became part of a great convoy heading for the airport of Mitiga. No waiting, no formalities whatsoever. The gates were wide open and the cars went directly onto the tarmac to drop us at the foot of the steps of the plane. Half the plane was filled with girls in khaki, beige, and blue uniforms. Blue was reserved for the Special Forces, the real women soldiers—heads high, stares icy, their training evident. Or so I was told. Like Amal, I wore khaki. A fake soldier. A real slave. In the back of the aircraft I noticed Jalal, and I was happy. The Guide was traveling in a different plane.

We disembarked in Bamako, the capital of Mali, and I could never have imagined the welcome we received—pure frenzy! The red carpet was laid down for Gaddafi, who strutted out in a white suit with a green map of Africa sewn over the chest. The president of Mali, various ministers, and a host of officials were competing to pay their respects to the "King of kings of Africa." And there was the crowd—joyful, excited, almost in ecstasy, singing, screaming, dancing, and shouting, "Welcome, Muammar!" There were folklore groups, traditional dancers, and people wearing Dogon masks, all of them shaking and swaying. I couldn't believe my eyes. Mabrouka quickly took control of the situation and signaled us to assemble at one side and get into a group of 4x4s that were ready to take us away, driven by our usual Libyan chauffeurs. It seemed that all of Bab al-Azizia was on the move. The crowd had gathered on the route of the convoy and kept on waving and chanting Gaddafi's name. I was flabbergasted. How was it possible for him to be so loved? I wondered. Were they sincere? Or were they as brainwashed as everyone in Libya?

We arrived at the Libya Hotel, where Sana, a woman from the Department of Protocol, made us wait in a room where we were able to smoke quietly. And then we left again in a convoy. Almost a hundred vehicles, tents, and food—utterly insane logistics. The roads were blocked off, the Africans were applauding as we passed, and the girls inside the cars were laughing. It was a cheerful atmosphere, almost like a carnival. I felt like I was at the movies. But while we were smiling back at the crowds that greeted us, I couldn't help but think how madly ironic a situation this was. We'd been let out of our basement to be shown off in the sun and contribute to his glory!

I had no idea what our destination was, or who the presidents, ministers, and ambassadors whom we met were. No idea of the Guide's personal affairs. We followed, like a royal entourage, without asking any questions. The early part of the journey was grueling, for we drove almost a thousand kilometers from the north to the south of Guinea to Conakry, the capital. The only thing the girls around me were curious about was where we would stay. They were hoping for luxury hotels with nightclubs and swimming pools. But it quickly became clear to me that I wouldn't have that luck. While Amal and the others went off to a hotel, Mabrouka signaled for me to follow the master, who was staying in an official residence, a kind of château. I had to share my room with Affaf, another girl, but in the middle of the night I was summoned to the Guide. He wasn't sleeping, was pacing naked around his room, looking somber and anxious. He kept turning, picking up his red towel, wiping his hands on it, concentrating and ignoring my presence. At dawn, he finally hurled himself at me.

During the day I met up with the rest of the group—Amal, Jalal, and all the others. They were in a magnificent hotel and the atmosphere was festive. I'd never seen anything like this before. Mabrouka had demanded that I go back to the château at night, but I couldn't help following everyone else to the nightclub. With bright colored lights shining on them, the girls were smoking and drinking alcohol, dancing close with African men. Sirte and my family seemed very far away. I'd landed on a planet where there was no room for the values and beliefs of my parents. Where my survival depended solely on qualities or activities they abhorred. A planet where everything was upside down.

Jalal was watching me from afar. I caught his eye, and that was enough to make me happy. But he approached and advised me, "Soraya, the most important thing is that you shouldn't drink," which I really liked. He was sweet. The girls, on the other hand, kept on trying to convince me to drink. The music grew louder and louder; the club was packed, the atmosphere heated. Jalal kissed me. It was all completely unbelievable.

I slept at the hotel, in the room of one of the girls. Someone had called Mabrouka to ask for permission for me to stay away that night and, surprisingly, she allowed it. The master must have been busy. There were so many women who had followed him, and I know he collected more along the way. But the next morning it was action stations. "Uniforms, everyone at the ready, everything immaculate," the protocol woman yelled. "The Guide is going to give a speech in a huge stadium. Everyone must play their part!" The 4x4s brought us to the Conakry stadium, which was filling up with hordes of people, young and old, families with children. There were orchestras, banners, and people in splendid suits and boubous. Before leading us to the official stage, Nuri Mesmari, the chief of protocol, spoke to us: "You are not soldiers, but you must act as if you were really in charge of the Guide's security. Put yourself inside the skin of actual bodyguards. Look serious, focused, and attentive to everything that's happening around you." So I played at being a guard, mimicking Zohra, who had a forbidding expression on her face and looked around as if she were searching for terrorists.

When we came into the stadium, when I heard the roar of voices and saw the throng of more than fifty thousand people who were applauding Gaddafi and singing his praises, it took my breath away. Clusters of women were shouting his name and trying to get near him, touch his clothing, or even kiss him. It was wild. "You poor things," I said to myself. "You'd do better not to be noticed. He is a dangerous man." I was thinking of Mama, who might be seeing me on national television and would surely be moved, despite her loathing of Gaddafi. Maybe she'd say to herself that on this one day, at least, I was experiencing something pretty significant. But I thought of my brothers as well. What did they know? What would they think? That thought frightened me. I turned my head away and tried to hide my face. Their likely reaction made my blood run cold.

Gaddafi seemed bolstered by the crowd. He was calling out to them, smiling and laughing with them. He swelled with pride, shaking his fist like an athletic champion or the master of the universe. The other girls were fascinated, but I can assure you that I was not. Not for a second. This is what I saw written on his forehead, between his brown cap and his black sunglasses: "sick, mad, and dangerous."

And on we went, driving for hours more to the Ivory Coast via Sierra Leone. At the next hotel I had to share my room with Farida and Zohra, which was no problem since the bed was enormous. Everyone was happy and getting ready for the swimming pool. I was dying to go swimming, never having seen a hotel pool like that. But the Colonel could call for me at any moment. "Just say you have your period," Farida told me. "You know it's the one thing he's afraid of. But watch out, they do check! Put some lipstick on a pad." I thought that was pretty clever. Two hours later Fatiha ordered me in her deep voice to go to the Guide's residence. I put on a worried look and assured her I was much too tired. She raised her eyebrows as if I were trying to fool her. "I have my period."

"Really now! Let me see."

"You're not actually going to check me out?"

"Show me!"

It was a humiliating action, but the sight of the pad, sprinkled with water and colored with lipstick, convinced her, and Farida went to the Guide by herself.

So, liberated and lighthearted, I joined the other girls—and Jalal—in the pool. There was music; there were drinks and hookahs. No one was confiding in anyone but it felt like a kind of small rebellion. For a few hours we were allowed some luxury. We were part of Gaddafi's community, no longer the subhumans he saw us as, and the hotel staff attended to everyone's needs. For once there was a small compensation for our daily suffering and humiliations, though it was just a fleeting illusion. But it served as a safety valve, and much later on I understood that these rather infrequent moments kept some of us from giving up on life entirely.

Suddenly I heard someone shout: "Soraya!" Fatiha had spotted me. She came toward me, beside herself. "You are supposed to have your period and you're in the swimming pool?" I felt so sheepish that I couldn't find anything to say. Then she hit me. "Liar!" Farida had betrayed me. I was brought to the residence immediately. The master's punishment, they warned me, would match my trickery. But as I was waiting in a small room, Galina came to see me. "Soraya! How could you let yourself be fooled like that? Papa Muammar is in a rage and has ordered me to inspect you . . . My poor little love. You're putting me in a horrible position. What am I going to tell him?" Nothing. She said nothing. Or rather, she lied to him to protect me. They left me alone the rest of the day.

The next day we continued on the final leg of our trip, traveling to Ghana for the meeting of the heads of state of the African Union in Accra. We were on the road for hours and hours, a journey that never seemed to end. The second night Fatiha came to "inspect" me. No trace of any period. She stared at me coldly, said nothing, but alerted Mabrouka, who gave me an enormous slap before bringing me to Gaddafi. What's the use of going into detail? He slapped me, beat me up, spat on me, insulted me. I came out with a swollen face and they locked me up in a room, while Galina, I later heard, was instantly sent back to Libya. Mabrouka taunted me from the doorway: "You wanted to escape, did you? No matter where you may go one day, Muammar will find you again, and he'll kill you."

7

HICHAM

The trip through Africa didn't represent the end of my suffering, but it was the end of my total confinement. Was the Guide
getting tired of me? Had I passed my expiration date? I don't
know. There never was any logic or explanation. I lived from
day to day, depending on his goodwill, no horizon in sight. But
the day he returned from his African tour he had Mabrouka
call me in and with a pout of disgust tossed out these words
at me: "I don't want you anymore, you slut! I'm going to have
you join the revolutionary guards. You'll be living with them.
So get lost!"

After this, Mabrouka gave me a cell phone: "If you feel like
contacting your mother . . ." It came as a total surprise! I immediately called Mama. She had noticed me on national television in uniform behind Gaddafi in the stadium in Conakry

and seemed almost happy to let me know this. "How I'd love to see you, my darling. I miss you so much!" I felt emboldened enough to make another request of Mabrouka and against all expectations she answered that Mama could come by the following day to see me. At Bab al-Azizia!

Imagining her coming into this universe was, of course, sort of terrifying to me. But I needed her so much, so I explained how to get to the garage, the point from where someone would bring her to the Guide's residence. I was hoping that everyone would be nice to her. How naïve I could still be! Mabrouka, Salma, and Fatiha were downright obnoxious and callous. "You want to see your daughter? It's downstairs." Fortunately, Amal kissed her and let me know she was there, and I ran into her arms, where I immediately broke down crying and wept for a long time. I couldn't even get a word out. What would I tell her? Where would I start? This basement told my story for me. My sobs must have been unbearable. Mabrouka made fun of my tears, and Mama was hurt by that. And soon we were separated.

A few days later Galina appeared in my room, her face drained of color. The Guide ordered us to come to him together, wanting to know more about the African incident. I was bowled over that he had no more important topics to concern himself with.

"Why did you lie to me saying she had her period?" he asked the nurse.

"I didn't lie. In young girls the cycle can be quite irregular and their period can be slight."

"You're nothing but a liar, and deceitful to boot! Farida told me the truth. As for you, you little whore, go down to your room. You won't miss anything by waiting."

That was the last time I saw Galina at Bab al-Azizia. Very much later, at the beginning of the revolution, I would be astounded to see her on television, filmed at the time of her return to the Ukraine, the secret of her experience in Libya buried deep inside her. A few days after that stormy interview, Gaddafi sent for me again, and assaulted my body with such violence that I came out of it all groggy and covered in bruises. Amal G., another girl in the house also named Amal who was usually rather indifferent to my lot, was overcome. "I need to get you out of here for a while!" I didn't even pick up on it; I had no hope left, the days went by, and I was slowly going under. But she came back to my room with a triumphant look. "Mabrouka says it's all right for me to take you home to my family!" And she took me away for a few days to her place, or rather to her family's home, where her mother and her little sister were waiting for her with a heaping plate of couscous.

Three days later she was again given permission to take me out. Even though it was conditional, this freedom was incredible, and I didn't know what to make of my jailers' change of face. But the few hours outside of the compound gave me such a boost that I never asked any questions. I wasn't even thinking of escaping anymore. I had no hopes, no dreams. I was a long-forgotten girl, without any sort of future beyond Bab al-Azizia. One of those women, among so many others, who belonged to their master forevermore.

On that day I couldn't foresee that another man would come into my life.

Amal G. took me out to lunch in the old fishermen's quarter near the sea. We were about to leave and she was taking a step backward when a man yelled: "Watch out!" Looking exasperated, he came out of his car, which we'd almost smashed into. But he quickly calmed down. We exchanged a look, a smile, and that was it. I was head over heels. I didn't even know that feeling existed. An earthquake, with a before and an after. He was about thirty, with a square build, robust, muscular, his gaze as dark as his hair, and laden with energy. Better yet: with boldness. I was stunned. But Amal G. drove off, straight back to Bab al-Azizia, and life returned to its usual routine between the basement and the master's bedroom, between indolence and submission.

One afternoon I was permitted to go out with her again. She wanted to take her younger sister to a fair and show me the rides. One of them looked like a huge sieve, inside of which riders sat in a circle and held on to the edge, and then the whole thing shook in every direction. We were laughing and screaming, trying to keep our balance, when I realized that the man in charge of the ride was the one we'd seen the other day. Again our eyes crossed, and he increased the speed of the ride. Fear and excitement! The more I laughed as I clung to the side, the more he intensified the shaking. "We've seen each other before, haven't we?" he yelled.

"Yes, I remember. What's your name?"

"Hicham. Do you have a phone number?"

This was crazy! Completely forbidden and totally fabulous! He didn't have any paper but told me his number, which I dialed immediately so that he'd have mine in his phone. Amal G. quickly hauled me off elsewhere.

As I was returning to Bab al-Azizia I felt a sweet euphoria. Life was taking on a new hue. I called him from my room, which I knew was crazy. He picked up right away.

"Where are you?" he asked.

"At home."

"It was great to see you again at the fair. Nice coincidence, right?"

"I would have recognized you anywhere."

"I'd really like to see you again. What do you do in life?"

Oh, that question! I should have expected it. How could I answer it? I didn't do anything in life. I wasn't making anything of my life. In fact, I had no life. An abyss. I burst into tears.

"Nothing. I do absolutely nothing."

"Why are you crying? Tell me!"

"I can't."

In tears, I hung up the phone. I was eighteen years old now. The girls at my school had graduated. Some of them were already married. Others had been accepted to the university. I remembered how in middle school I'd dreamed of becoming a dentist. Teeth and smiles were the first thing I looked at in people and I couldn't keep myself from giving advice on how to take care of one's teeth, keep them clean and white. A dentist! It was almost laughable. What fun they'd make of me if I told that to people in my basement. They had ruined my dreams, stolen my life, and I couldn't even talk about it. For what they'd done to me was so shameful that, outside these walls, it was me who became the leper. What could I tell Hicham?

I didn't even have time enough to ponder the question. They called me upstairs.

"Get undressed, whore!" the Guide ordered when I got to his bedroom.

This time I felt it went too far. I burst out in sobs. "Why do you say that to me? Why? I'm not a whore!" That enraged him. He roared "Shut your mouth, whore" and raped me, making me understand that I was nothing but a possession of his, someone without any right to speak. When I went back down to my room I saw on the cell phone I had hidden under my pillow that Hicham had called me twenty-five times. At least there was someone who saw me as a person.

The next night Gaddafi summoned me again and abused me once more. Then he forced me to snort cocaine. I didn't want to; it scared me. My nose started bleeding and he put some on my tongue. I blacked out.

I woke up with an oxygen mask on my face in the infirmary of the Ukrainians. Elena was caressing my hand and another nurse, Alina, was watching me anxiously. They didn't say a word but I could see they were worried about me. They brought me back to my room, where I spent two days in bed, unable to stand. The only thing that kept me alive was thinking about Hicham.

Amal G. didn't find out what had happened to me until the next day. Though I was doing a little better I was in no mood to talk, but she took me by the hand and dragged me to the Guide. He was sitting in front of his computer. "Master! You're not seriously giving drugs to this young one! It's criminal. And dangerous. What's come over you?" She was confronting him with astonishing audacity. Her hand in mine, the other on her hip, she was demanding an answer. She had dared to confront him! "Get the hell out!" he shouted, showing her the door. "And leave her here!"

He jumped on me, crushing my chest, and yelled "Dance!" as he put on the music. Then he pinned me to the floor: "Why did you talk, you slut?"

"I said nothing. They guessed it on their own."

He beat me and raped me, urinated on me, and as he went to take a shower he screamed: "Go away!" I went back downstairs, wet and wretched, convinced that no shower would ever wash me clean again.

Amal G. stayed angry. And yet she had a true fascination with the Guide. Maybe she even loved him, as implausible as that seemed to me. She said that she was indebted to him for the house her family owned, for her car, for a comfortable life. I asked no questions; I hated him far too much. But when she said, "I swear it on Muammar's head," I knew I could believe her. She didn't hesitate to put everyone at Bab al-Azizia in their place. She'd yell at the horrible Saada Al Fallah, one of the heads of the Department of Protocol, who called her a whore: "You'd do better to be quiet, you fag!" She'd shout and swear, as friendly as a porcupine, not caring at all about the others. But my distress worried her. In the morning she came into my room and said: "Come, I'm taking you home with me. They've given me permission. Bring enough things for a few days."

I threw my arms around her, kissed her. "All right, all right," she said as she released herself, always a little aloof, but I could see she had tears in her eyes. So we left to go to her family's house. How sweet it was at first, that impression of a normal family life: a house, parents, regular meals. I felt homesick for my own family and phoned Mama. "You have to come get me." Amal G. hit the roof. "Don't say you're at my house! You absolutely can't! If you tell your mother, I'm taking you back to Bab al-Azizia immediately." She scared me. Anything but returning to my basement, seeing Gaddafi and Mabrouka again. Anything, including lying to Mama, something I'd never done before.

That's when I discovered the strange secret life of Amal G., the network she had built up to obtain alcohol, her nocturnal car trips, her friendliness with the police officers who crossed her path—"How is it going, Amal?"—and the mixture of Red Bull and vodka she'd drink at the wheel before she'd splash perfume on herself on her way back. It became clear to me she was hungry for money, and had dealings with businessmen who sent commissions her way. And I realized fairly quickly she was using me to attract powerful and wealthy men. She took me and other girls to parties that were eagerly attended by the country's dignitaries and celebrities, where an abundance of alcohol and drugs was available, and where money circulated in exchange for sexual favors. Was that all they wanted from me? Was my body, which I despised, really the only thing I had to offer? Was that all I was worth, even outside the harem? Did my link to Bab al-Azizia raise my value in the eyes of certain men? A single night at the opulent home of a famous cousin of Gaddafi's earned me five thousand dinars—money which Amal G. quickly pocketed and I never dared ask for. She had me in her power.

One day, when I was on the phone with Mama, catching up on her news, she told me that Inas, my childhood friend from Benghazi, was in Tripoli and really wanted to see me again. She gave me Inas's number, which I called right away. I really wanted to pick up the thread with normal people, people from my earlier life, although I didn't know whether that was even possible anymore. Inas answered promptly and very enthusiastically. I asked for her address, suggesting that I come see her right there and then. "Oh, really? You can leave Bab al-Azizia?" She knew! I was dumbfounded. How did Mama dare tell her the truth when she'd been lying to the entire family from the start?

I took a taxi and asked Inas to pay the driver when I got there. "How can it be that a girl who's living at the president's house has no money to pay for her cab?" she joked. I smiled but didn't answer. How much did she know? What did "living at the president's house" mean to her? Did she think it was my choice? A status symbol and a real job? I was going to have to walk on eggshells.

We went into the house and the whole family greeted me with hugs and kisses. "We'll call your mother so she can join us," Inas said, suddenly very excited.

"No!"

"Why not?"

"You shouldn't . . . I'm temporarily with another girl, outside Bab al-Azizia, who doesn't want people to know."

Everyone looked at me skeptically, in silence. So little Soraya was lying to her mother. And that ruined the atmosphere. "What is your relationship to Bab al-Azizia?" someone asked.

"I don't want to talk about that. Surely Mama told you my story."

Then I lit a cigarette, causing a mixture of dismay and disapproval in the family's eyes. Soraya sure had turned out badly.

I spent the night there. It was a break for me, a brief return to childhood, and it was lovely. Amal G. must have been crazy with anger and worry—I hadn't accepted a single one of her many calls. When I finally did answer the next morning, she shouted at me.

"How could you go out without alerting me?"

"I needed some air, can't you understand that? At your place I feel imprisoned all over again. Thank you for getting me out of Bab al-Azizia, but now let me breathe a little."

She kept on yelling, I started to cry, and then Inas picked up the phone. "I am a childhood friend of hers, and my family is taking care of her, don't worry." But Amal G. insisted and said that I was putting myself in a terribly dangerous situation whose consequences I wasn't taking into consideration. So in the end Inas gave her address to Amal G. "I'm coming!" she said. That was what I had been afraid of. The only refuge I had left, the one that nobody at Bab al-Azizia would have known about, was going to be discovered. I felt hunted. So I called Hicham. "I beg you, please come get me. I don't want to see anyone but you anymore."

He got there in a few minutes and all but kidnapped me. The car tore through the streets of Tripoli, then through the suburbs and into the countryside. He was tense at the wheel, focused on the road. I was watching his profile, my head back against the seat and more relaxed than I had been in ages. I wasn't thinking any thoughts; I had no plan; I was smiling, simply trusting this man whom I'd met only twice before. I had made no mistake. He was strong and spirited. He drove me to a small vacation house and said: "Get some rest. I know your story and from now on I won't let anyone hurt you." Without my knowledge, Amal G. had gone to see him to tell him what my connection was with Bab al-Azizia, saying: "This is no girl for you." And there she was calling me on my cell phone, having tried a dozen times already. "Pick up," Hicham said. "You don't need to be afraid of her anymore. Tell her the truth."

Trembling, I picked up. She exploded: "You are insane, Soraya! You're really looking for trouble. How dare you escape when I was coming to get you?"

"Leave me alone! I'm far away, staying with a girlfriend."

"You're lying! I know you're with Hicham!"

I hung up. Hicham took the phone from me and called her back. "Leave her in peace. Forget her. You've hurt her enough. From now on I'll defend her. And I'm quite capable of killing if anyone tries to harm her."

"You don't know me, Hicham. You'll pay very dearly for this. I'll make sure you end up in prison."

For three days I was happy. The first twenty-four hours I did nothing but cry—I think I was just crying the overflow of five years' worth of tears. Hicham was patient, gentle, soothing. He prepared food for me, cleaned up, wiped my tears away, and finally I was no longer alone. Perhaps there was life after Bab al-Azizia after all.

But at the Gaddafi house the news of my escape exploded. Amal G. had taken Inas to my mother, who called me immediately: "I'm crushed, Soraya. You've been lying to me for two months! How is that possible? You're in the city, you smoke, you run away with a man. What has become of my little Soraya? A slut! A whore! It would be better to see you dead than to imagine you living this life. I am so disappointed in you!" I took the blow. The way things looked was against me. But how could she not see that I was just trying to survive?

Amal G. called me again: "Whatever you do, you'll come back to Bab al-Azizia eventually." And sure enough, the internal security forces in their 4x4s besieged the home of Hicham's parents: "Where is your son? He must bring back the girl he kidnapped." His brothers phoned him in a panic. So after three days we gave up.

I went to Amal G., who gave me a choice: to be taken to my parents or to Bab al-Azizia. I chose my parents, but with great anxiety. I could tell that our bond of trust had been broken. Mama stared at me long and hard, as if my face had become a mirror of my depravity, as if I was no longer her poor stolen child but a guilty daughter, a fallen girl. My father welcomed me more affectionately. He looked me over carefully, seeming to not quite recognize me. I think I'd grown a little, but most of all I had aged. Still, he had to play the father's role and quickly began to ask for an explanation. Who was this Hicham? I told him how lucky I'd been to have had this chance encounter, about his courage, his cool-headedness, and his gentlemanly manners, and about his wish to marry me. They listened to me with a look of disbelief. There was a distance between us that had never been there before.

My mother didn't want me leaving the house anymore, more out of fear of this new danger, Hicham, than of Bab al-Azizia. I had to resort to a subterfuge, pretending I was accompanying Papa somewhere and giving him the slip long enough to see Hicham, who provided me with cigarettes and a new card for my cell phone. This way neither Amal G. nor Mabrouka could call me again. At home the atmosphere was tense. It almost killed me not to be able to smoke and sometimes I would hide in the bathroom to have a cigarette, then use an air freshener afterward. I had nothing to talk about. It was as if I were hanging in the air.

Then one morning at dawn I heard a knock at the door. It was the driver from Bab al-Azizia. "Come with me, Soraya, you are wanted over there."

So I left again. Icily, Mabrouka led me to the little lab, where a nurse took three vials of blood from me. I had to wait for an hour in a small room before Salma snarled: "Go upstairs!" The Guide was waiting for me in a jogging suit and a sleeveless T-shirt. "What a slut! I know you slept with other men." He spat in my face, fucked me, and urinated on me, then concluded: "There's only one solution left for you: to work under my command. You will sleep at home, but from nine in the morning until nine at night I want you here, at my disposal. You will finally learn to have the discipline of the revolutionary guards."

8

ESCAPE

The next morning a driver from Bab al-Azizia rang my parents' doorbell at eight-thirty sharp. I was going to work, going to be a guard. I didn't know what that was supposed to consist of and just hoped it meant I wouldn't have any further contact with the Guide. What did a "revolutionary guard" actually do? How was I going to defend the revolution? The answer came very quickly: by serving drinks all day long to the Guide's African guests! I was in the same house with the same people and the same mistress of the house as before! And at three o'clock in the morning I was still there. "This isn't what the Guide told me I'd be doing," I complained to Mabrouka.

"Maybe not. And what's more, you'll be spending the night right here."

But I no longer had a room. A new girl had taken my place. So I got ready to sleep on one of the couches in the living room, as if I were just passing through. As soon as the last of the Africans left, I was summoned upstairs to the Guide, together with the new girl. None of this was "revolutionary." I was as trapped as before.

The next day I called my father on the sly. It was a short conversation; I could tell he was nervous. "Soraya, this is important. Join me as fast as you can with your passport." I still had it! It was amazing but I still had it. Carelessness on Mabrouka's part when we returned from the African journey. I told one of the drivers that I had to run a pressing errand, asked him to wait for me for a moment, and then jumped in a cab to meet Papa, who was waiting for me in his car. He took off and drove me to the French Embassy to submit an application for an emergency visa; they had needed a photograph and my fingerprints. With a little luck and an old connection of my father's at the embassy, they assured us that it would be ready in a week instead of a month. Less than an hour later, after taking small alleyways, avoiding the bigger roads, and looking in his rearview mirror a thousand times, Papa dropped me off in a taxi that took me back to the driver, and I returned to Bab al-Azizia.

The next day I was again playing the waitress role. The house was filled with famous people, even stars I recognized: a film director and a singer from Egypt, a Lebanese singer, dancers and television hosts. The Guide came out of his office to join them in the grand reception hall and sat down with them. Then he went upstairs to his bedroom. And quite a few of them joined him there, one after another. An overstuffed Samsonite waited for each of them before they departed.

I could go home to my parents' house, but I understood quickly enough that I no longer belonged there. I was a stranger. A bad example for everyone. Now quite distant toward me, Mama spent most of her time in Sirte with my sister and my youngest brother, the two older ones having left to study abroad. So only Papa and my other two brothers were now living in Tripoli. But living with my parents didn't work. In fact, it was a real disaster. "What kind of a life is this?" Papa would ask. "What sort of an example for your brothers and the rest of the family?" It was so much simpler when they didn't see me. I would have been less of an embarrassment if I were dead. So something unimaginable happened—I began to prefer life at Bab al-Azizia to being at home.

Back to the lab. Blood test. Makeshift bed in the living room while waiting to be called for during the night. Then Papa phoned me: "Be ready. In four days you'll have your visa for France." So, taking my courage in both hands, I went to confront Gaddafi. "My mother is very sick. I'll need three weeks off." He gave me two. I went home again. But what an atmosphere! I had to hide to smoke cigarettes and phone Hicham, and I was getting on everyone's nerves. I lied, pretending they'd called me back to Bab al-Azizia again, and went to meet my lover. I knew that this was serious, that I was out of my mind, but a little more, a little less . . . My whole life had gone off the tracks a long time ago! Lying became a way to survive.

I spent two days with Hicham in a bungalow lent to him by a friend. "I love you," he said. "You can't just leave me like this."

"It's the only solution. I can't live in Libya anymore. Bab al-Azizia will never leave me alone and my family sees me as a kind of monster. And I'll only cause you trouble."

"Why can't you wait so we can go abroad together?"

"No. Here I'll always be hounded and put you in danger. My only hope to have Gaddafi forget me is to leave."

I went home to pack my suitcase, moving like a sleepwalker, indifferent to everything happening around me. I'd been told that February in France was very harsh and that I would need real shoes and a really warm coat. In a closet, I found a stack of clothes that Mama had bought for me when she went to Tunisia. "That's for Soraya," she'd told my father. "I'm sure she'll be coming back this year." Mama . . . She'd been waiting for me to return for five years. During the day she'd face up to the insidious questions and keep the family firmly in hand. At night she would sob and pray to God to protect her little girl and bring her back safely. But I was not a little girl anymore, and I had disappointed her.

Papa made me get up very early. His face was white. No, really it was green, but his lips were white. I had never seen him like that before—he was scared stiff. He had used gel to comb his hair back. He was wearing a dark suit I didn't recognize underneath a leather jacket. The smoky sunglasses completed the picture to make him look like a gangster or a spy. I quickly slipped on a pair of jeans and a shirt, and wrapped myself in a black veil and sunglasses that made my face disappear. I called Mama to say goodbye. It was a short, cold phone call. Then we grabbed a cab for the airport. Papa kept throwing me irritated glances. "What's wrong with you, Soraya? You look as if you don't give a damn!" Oh, no, I did give a damn. But I was calm. What could possibly happen to me that was more serious than what I'd already lived through? Get killed? That would have been a relief.

At the airport Papa was on his guard. He was looking at his watch, and became jumpy as soon as anyone brushed past him; I was afraid he was about to have a heart attack. He had asked a friend to take care that my name wouldn't appear on the passenger list, not even my initials. He checked that again. As we passed through security and then went into the departure lounge, he threw anxious glances in all directions, suspicious that any solitary passenger was one of Gaddafi's henchmen. He was in a spy film. Until the moment we took off, he just stared at the front door of the airplane, unable to speak. His mouth was dry, and his hands clutched the armrest until we reached Rome. As if an order from the Guide could still turn the plane around. But then when we landed, he laughed—for the first time in several years, he admitted.

He had chosen an itinerary through Rome just to confuse things. As we had a layover of a few hours, I went to the bathroom to get rid of the black veil I was wearing and put on some eyeliner, a bit of lip gloss, and some perfume. We were going to Paris, the city of beauty and fashion. My wretched existence had come to an end.

Or, at least, so I thought.

9

PARIS

I dreamed of seeing the Eiffel Tower but, instead, we took the RER to the suburb of Kremlin-Bicêtre. I imagined an exotic scene but found myself surrounded by Arabs. "Is this France?" I asked my father, as we were going to meet one of his friends in a chain restaurant that served Halal chicken. I was disappointed. The cold was arctic, my nose and feet were frozen, everything seemed awful. "It will be nicer tomorrow," Papa said encouragingly. We spent the night in a small hotel at the Porte d'Italie from which you could see the beltway around Paris. And I woke up wanting to smoke, a habit which soon became a full-fledged addiction.

We had an appointment with Papa's friend Habib and went to wait for him in a nearby café. Girls were smoking on the terrace, relaxed and normal, which gave me some hope.

So it wasn't a defect or a vice, as they wanted me to think. I ordered hot chocolate, Papa ordered coffee, and even before they brought it to us he had gone out to smoke. There was no question of my keeping him company; he wouldn't have put up with it. So I dove into the restroom to smoke a Marlboro, a package of which I'd kept hidden. Habib arrived and invited us to his house at the Porte de Choisy. That's when Mama called. Soddeik, the driver from Bab al-Azizia, had stopped by the house in Tripoli: "Where is Soraya? Why doesn't her phone answer?" "Because she's in Sirte," they'd told him. The driver had accepted the answer, but Mama was extremely worried and my father began to shake. He was pale and in shock. Too many emotions. He collapsed in front of Habib and they took him to the hospital. He was discharged in the middle of the night, having decided to return to Tripoli straightaway. He gave me a thousand euros, which seemed like a fortune to me, and a telephone card, and asked Habib to rent a studio apartment for me. Then they went off to the airport together. Overwhelmed and anxious, he didn't kiss me, just gave me a small sign goodbye. "If God grants me life"—I knew that what he was thinking was, if they didn't kill him—"I'll send you more money." I cried as we said farewell.

Habib found me a room in a furnished hotel near the Porte de Choisy. It wasn't in the heart of Paris, but it wasn't so bad either. The receptionist was Moroccan, so she and I could speak Arabic together. I quickly mastered the bus and metro maps. One of my first orientation practice sessions landed me in the Latin Quarter, near the Saint-Michel metro stop, where I treated myself to a cup of coffee and watched the passersby. I was free. Free! I kept repeating it to myself without entirely believing it. I had no plans or schedule whatsoever. No friends, no network, but I was free. It was dizzying.

At the next table, two young girls and a man of Arabic origin were getting ready to party at a club, late at night. I was listening to them, envious and fascinated, and dying to approach them, but I didn't dare. This city, so elegant and yet so carefree, intimidated me. I went home.

The next morning I took the metro to the Champs-Elysées. That had been a dream of mine since I was a little girl. The sky was clear, the avenue even wider than I had imagined, and the Café Deauville precisely where Mama had said it was. I phoned her: "The Deauville is still blue!" I knew I was touching a sensitive spot in her. "You see how history repeats itself? My daughter is following in the tracks I made when I was twenty . . . How I'd like to be there with you, Soraya!" I headed for the Sephora department store, which I'd heard mentioned by Mabrouka, who did her shopping there. In the perfume department I tested every item, suspiciously watched by the security people. A saleswoman suggested I buy a small bottle of Paris but I had to do some calculations. I had a thousand euros; my hotel cost twenty-five euros a day, and I figured I needed twenty-five euros for food and transportation. My thousand euros would last me twenty days. So never mind the perfume. I'd really wanted to look around the makeup section too, but turned my back and decided I'd save it for another time. Eventually I would go through every aisle, since I had all the time in the world from now on.

It was the sight of a couple of young lovers, who were openly kissing, that made me think of Hicham. I had kept myself from calling him. What was the use? I was just a source of trouble. Still, I quickly went to buy credit for my international phone card, and as soon as I heard his voice I started to cry. "You've been gone for two days!" he said. "Two days in which I've been thinking of you constantly. I will join you as soon as I can. I've started the process of applying for a passport." So he was really serious? He wanted to live close to me? My God! I didn't want to wait any longer. Getting him that famous passport, a rare and precious object in Libya, had to be rushed through. And with money anything was possible. So I quickly called Papa: "You only left me a thousand euros. That's too little! How do you want me to manage with just that?" The next day he transferred two thousand euros, and I sent half of it to Hicham.

And then I had a whole series of encounters that, I realize today, led to the shipwrecking of my move to France, to its total failure. It's terrible to have to acknowledge that. It's so humiliating to admit that I let my chance go by. How is it possible? I placed my trust in the wrong people and made bad choices. I was frighteningly naïve. But there it is. I arrived in Paris in February of 2009, a few days before my twentieth birthday, knowing nothing of life, other than the spinelessness, perversity, and

negativity of the small world that had imprisoned me. I had no
idea of the working world, of relations within society, of time
and money management, of balanced relationships between
men and women. And nothing about the ways of the world. I
had never even read a newspaper . . .

I was sitting on a bench on the Champs-Elysées when a
young blonde woman sat down next to me. "Hi. Is there any
room?"

"Of course. What's your name?"

"Warda."

"That's an Arabic name!"

She was of Algerian origin, and we rapidly became friendly.
"I can tell that you have just arrived in Paris. Where are you
from?"

"Guess!"

"Morocco?"

"No. From a country you would never think of."

"Tunisia? Egypt? Jordan? Lebanon?"

"No! A strategically important country in North Africa.
So?!"

"From Algeria? Like me?"

"No!"

"Well, then I don't know."

"From Libya!"

"Ah! Gaddafi! Brilliant! That guy is one of my heroes. You
have no idea how fascinating I find him! Tell me all about
him!"

"You admire Gaddafi?" I felt like crying. "But he's a crook! An impostor!"

"Are you kidding? Have you heard his speeches? Did you see how he defied America? He is a true Arab! And he has such charisma!"

We continued the conversation in a café, where her friend found us. He was a security guard at La Marquise, a club in Montreuil. Since they were planning to go there that evening they suggested that I come as well. I liked that idea. "What luck!" I said to myself. It was a Lebanese restaurant that changed into a nightclub after midnight, with an orchestra and a belly dancer. Oh, I sure felt at home, with everyone speaking Arabic, while the public, which was joyful, extroverted, very eager to party, seemed to consist of wealthy Asians. "Look to your right," Warda suddenly signaled me. "Some men at the next table are watching you."

"So what? In that case I definitely don't want to look!"

"Be nice! If you are gracious they'll pay for your drinks and food. Come and dance."

Reluctantly, I followed her. Where was she dragging me? Some of the men followed us onto the dance floor, flirting and growing ever more audacious, some even slipping us bills, as one does with professional dancers. I rushed over to Warda: "Come. I don't want anything to do with this!" But the owner noticed me and came over: "Is it true that you are Libyan?" Then he picked up the mike and said: "Ladies and gentlemen, I would like to salute Libya and Colonel Gaddafi!" I turned to jelly, but the guy continued: "So come on, come help me sing a song to the glory of the Colonel!" And in front of the microphone he crooned one of those monstrous songs that the loudspeakers and radio regularly spewed forth in Libya: "Oh, our Guide, it is you we follow . . ." I just wanted to disappear. Could he possibly catch up with me here? I ran to the restroom and locked myself in to cry.

I stayed cloistered in my room for a week, completely devastated. I went out only to buy cigarettes and credit for my phone card. I woke up in anguish; Gaddafi's shadow pursued me wherever I went. Bab al-Azizia had eyes and ears across the entire planet. His spies had already murdered people at the other end of the world. So . . . was it realistic to expect I could get away from his clutches? Only barely after arriving in Paris I already felt I'd reached a dead end. And then one night a rat ran across my room. That was a shock. I packed up and left the room, hurried to reception, paid my bill, and in a panic called Habib.

"Spend the night here and we'll see what we'll do in the next few days."

I went to his house and he put me up in a room, but around four in the morning he slipped into my bed. Papa's friend! I screamed, grabbed my bag, and tore down the stairs. The street was deserted and it was freezing outside. Where could I go? I thought of Warda and dialed her number. No answer. I walked to the metro and waited for the station to open so I could sit down on a bench. There some drunk tramp started to harass me. I was crying. I rang Hicham's number but there was no answer. My father's friend kept calling me like a madman.

I emerged from the metro station and dove into the café at the Porte de Choisy, which had just opened. I ordered coffee and then, suddenly, a dozen or so policemen came in to check the place. I panicked. Warda had warned me: "Above all else, don't let them check up on you!" I couldn't escape; they came toward me and I handed them my passport, trembling all the while. One of the officers, a Moroccan, smiled. "Why are you so scared? You have a visa, your papers are in fine order!" I was paralyzed, incapable of saying a word. He slipped me his phone number with a vulgar wink. I was disgusted.

A group of self-confident, elegant girls came into the café. Undoubtedly they worked together in one of the office buildings, and I watched them in fascination. "Really," I thought, "these Frenchwomen have such class! They're always nicely turned out, they dress smartly, go out and smoke in cafés, and have jobs that are just as important as those of their male counterparts." But then one of them came up to me and shouted: "Why are you staring at me like that? Do you have a problem?" Oh, that phrase! It stays with me still even though I didn't understand her meaning right away. Her face expressed such scorn and hate. Why was she telling me off like that? I was only admiring her, and if I myself looked terrible it was because I hadn't slept all night.

The barman was kind. He spoke Arabic, too. "I have to learn French," I told him. "It's really important." He advised me to go to the Alliance française in Montparnasse and jotted down the address on a piece of paper. I took the metro, suitcase in hand, got off beneath the Montparnasse Tower, got lost, and was surprised to see that no one spoke Arabic in this district. I sat down in a café, and whom did I see? Habib! He worked in the neighborhood. "Why aren't you answering your phone, Soraya? I was worried sick!"

"Don't ever say my name again. Leave me alone or I'm calling Papa."

He found a chair and sat down across from me. "Be nice! I'm going to help you. I'm going to find you work and a residence permit."

"Get the hell away. Or better yet, take me to the Alliance française."

It was very close by. Inside a group of Algerian women was very busy discussing the fees for the courses and which arrondissements had classes that were free of charge. One of them even offered to drive me to the town hall of the sixth arrondissement. The waiting room was full of Arabs and Africans. "You're in luck," a teacher said to me. "There's a class that's just begun. Go on in, quick!" At the blackboard a woman was in the middle of having the class recite the letters of the alphabet on the board. A-B-C-D-E . . . I'd known these letters since middle school in Sirte. If I had to start from scratch it would take months and I wouldn't be any closer to

116

managing the outside world—a thought too discouraging to bear!

At that moment Warda called. I told her I was out on the street. "Come move in with me," she said spontaneously. "I live alone with my little boy." And so I found myself temporarily with a roof above my head (Porte de Montreuil), a friend (a sometime club hostess), and a neighborhood (Arabic-speaking). It was reassuring at first, though it would ruin me in the end.

From the first night on, Warda wanted to take me to La Marquise. Initially I refused, but I was afraid to find myself homeless again. At the club she introduced me to an elegant and kind Tunisian man named Adel, who instantly fell in love with me. I made it very clear to him that I loved another man and would remain faithful to him. He made do with coming to La Marquise as often as he could, treating us to dinner and drinks. Warda and her friends consumed large quantities of alcohol but I mostly had fruit juice. Hicham had made me swear on the Koran that I wouldn't ever touch a drop of alcohol again. And, crazily, that is how I spent the first three months of my time in Paris.

Then my tourist visa expired. And anxiety took over again. From then on I was on my guard everywhere I went—I didn't want to take any risks. I let Warda know I wouldn't go back to La Marquise anymore, but she laughed. "Oh, come on! All the girls at the club are in the same situation. The cops are too busy checking up on the guys and the vagrants to worry about you." I also started to need money, and my relationship with Warda deteriorated. She went so far as to keep me from touching what was in the refrigerator: "That's for my son!" I called Papa for help. "But how are you spending your money? Find a job, Soraya! Go wash dishes if you have to!" That hurt. "Well, if you want me to I'll go right back to Bab al-Azizia. It won't bother me!" He sent me five hundred euros, that was all. After a trip to the Carrefour supermarket with Warda, I soon had only one hundred euros left.

Then Adel suggested I could stay with him. He had a large apartment where I would have my own room, and we'd live together like friends. "Super," Warda said. "It's the ideal solution." What that meant, in short, was "Get out!"

So for six months I lived in Bagneux, near Paris. It was six months of relative tranquillity since Adel, who managed a small enterprise that handled different kinds of construction work, painting included, did his best to be a pleasant and respectful companion. He'd go to work in the morning, leaving me with fifty euros so I could eat and do the shopping. He knew I was in love with someone else, and I knew that saddened him, but we lived together in harmony. I trusted him, and when I told him of my drama at Bab al-Azizia he believed me right away; he had Libyan friends who had mentioned the abduction of schoolgirls to him. Warda had rejected my story right off the bat. I must have been an idiot to confide in her! She'd defend Gaddafi with the zeal of a believer, which made me sick to my stomach: "He is a credit to the Arabs, the only one to keep his head held high, to bear our torch! He is a Guide in the most glorious sense of the word, and a Guide wouldn't know how to act in a base fashion. It's revolting that you try to make yourself look interesting at his expense!" I couldn't bear listening to this.

Then one night, after coming home from a party in honor of his birthday at the Mazazic restaurant near the Place de la Nation, Adel came to my room with something pressing. I let him in. He had told his friends that he wanted to marry me. Or so I believe. But I remained firm: I wasn't free—my boyfriend would join me as soon as he had his passport, in just a few weeks.

Jealousy began to wear him down. One day while I was taking a shower he answered a call from Hicham on my cell phone. His voice grew louder and louder, until he was shouting. When I came in, beside myself, he hung up, screaming, "Son of a bitch!" I didn't take that betrayal well at all. What right did he have to answer my telephone? I called Hicham back but he said he wouldn't talk to me again. And I exploded in a rage. The situation had gone on way too long. I had to leave, and I had to find work.

An Egyptian I had met at the corner Tunisian grocery store introduced me to Manar, a Moroccan woman who worked in a bar-restaurant on a small street in Montreuil that was run by a Kabyle, a member of an Algerian ethnic group. They showed me how to make coffee and serve draft beer. I was earning fifty euros a day plus tips, which sometimes amounted to as much as a hundred euros! That was enough. All the more so since they proposed that I share the studio apartment upstairs with the Moroccan woman. I worked for a month and a half until I realized it was a shady place—the boss would sometimes close the curtains so the women could dance in the nude—and also that my housemate was stealing from me, something which drove me crazy. I took my things and left. Warda, with whom I'd stayed in touch, then put me in the hands of a Tunisian woman who worked in a bar at the Porte des Lilas in Paris. I started by washing dishes in the kitchen, then learned to wait tables and take orders. The Kabyle manager noticed that some customers kept coming back to see me and told me to work only in the dining area. That irritated the Tunisian woman. So one used me as bait, the other as a servant. One evening, I came back to the room I shared with another Moroccan girl and discovered that my things had been stolen again. I grabbed my suitcase and slammed the door behind me.

Once again I was on the street. I didn't know who else I could turn to. I thought of the Egyptian man. He welcomed me into the large apartment that he shared with several other people. He asked me no questions, but I felt ill at ease. I was dead weight. What was my future? What space could I expect to fill in Paris? I hadn't learned any French. My papers weren't in order and I ran the risk of being stopped at any time. I was not settling anything. That's when Hicham phoned. Just seeing his name on my cell phone gave me a smidgen of hope. He was thinking about me at the very moment the bottom was falling out for me. "When are you coming?" I asked. "I need you!"

"Never, you hear? Never! You couldn't even manage to be faithful to me!"

I was shattered and called my mother: "Everything is your fault! My life is in shambles. I'm totally lost, Mama. Lost! I don't know what to do, whom to trust, or where to go. I'm screwed. All because of you."

"Because of me?"

"I wouldn't have left if you'd accepted Hicham!"

"Oh, Soraya, don't say such foolish things. Just come home. France isn't working out for you. Come back to us."

The thought of going back to Libya hadn't even crossed my mind. Go back home? But I wasn't a tourist; I wasn't even a willing emigrant! I was on the run! And sought by one of the most powerful men in the world. It was all very well and good to let my aggression out on Mama, but the real reason for my departure was Gaddafi.

"But coming back would be so risky, Mama. They'll come and look for me. They'll never leave me in peace."

"We'll figure out a way to hide you. Your father had some trouble, but you can live with me in Sirte. At first they were really looking for you constantly, but I think they've calmed down. I don't want you being miserable in Paris."

And so my decision was made. In just a few seconds. Based on what passed through my head and a moment of the blues. I had no way of making a living in France; the country fascinated me but it wasn't my home. I didn't even know any French! I went to see Warda, who agreed I should go. But she did warn me: since my visa had expired I would need to pay a huge fine at the airport. To help me out, she called a friend who was a police officer at Roissy–Charles de Gaulle Airport. Three days later I would give him fifteen hundred euros so I wouldn't be prohibited from coming back into French territory again—at least that's how I understood it. Fortunately, Mama had sent me two thousand euros the night before.

On May 26, 2010, I took a plane back to Libya with an almost empty suitcase. Very few clothes, not a single book, not even a photograph. I had nothing left from the fifteen months I'd spent in the City of Light. Not even the small portrait some illustrator had made of me one spring evening at the foot of the Eiffel Tower, which Adel had kept as a souvenir.

10

COGWHEELS

No one was waiting for me at the Tripoli airport. I'd been very careful not to alert anyone at all. Not a single acquaintance in the arrival hall. No suspicious looks from any soldier or police officer. I was coming back incognito. Perhaps Bab al-Azizia had lowered its guard.

I called Hicham, who was blown away. "You're here? In Libya? Stay where you are, I'm on my way!" He came charging over in a 4x4 with two friends. He came out smiling and took my small case. Being affectionate or embracing in public was out of the question. But when I looked at Hicham, I immediately felt more confident. He had put on a bit of weight and seemed slightly older than I remembered him, and that made him all the more reassuring. We went to the same bungalow one of his friends had lent us before and talked things through. He had harsh words to explain how disappointed he was in me for having lived with another man in Paris. "He was just a friend," I insisted.

"Friendship is not possible between a man and a woman!"

There you had it. Typical Libyan male. Then he told me that the people from Bab al-Azizia had come looking for me at his parents' house. That they had imprisoned his brother while he himself had gone to Tunisia. That he had been the target of all sorts of harassment: he had received death threats, his telephone had been bugged, he had been tailed. He'd been denounced at work, and our relationship, widely known, had now earned him the label "lover of one of Gaddafi's whores." Even his close friends told him that he really couldn't marry a slut.

Then I grew scared. What about my parents? What had been done to them? What sorts of pressure, threats, punishments? Too busy with my own struggle to survive, I'd neglected them. How had the Guide made them pay for letting me escape? I wanted to see them right away. "Take me back to the airport," I said to Hicham. "I will call my parents and tell them I've just landed."

We drove in silence. From time to time he threw me a few sad glances, but I was absorbed in my own thoughts. How could I imagine that Bab al-Azizia would ever leave us alone? I called my parents, who were also astonished at my unexpected return, and then I sat down in the arrivals hall to wait for them. That's where I suddenly ran into Amal G., who was leaving for Tunisia with her older sister.

"Soraya! What a surprise! Where are you going? I heard you were in Paris."

"Not at all!"

"Don't lie to me. I did my investigating. I met Hicham, and a friend at the airport told me you had left."

"So much for solidarity!"

"You're wrong. I kept my information to myself. But you can imagine how furious Mabrouka and Muammar are . . ."

Papa arrived with my little sister, whom I hadn't seen in a very long time. He admitted that Bab al-Azizia had looked for me relentlessly and put all kinds of pressure on him to find me. But he said nothing more. Theoretically, my little sister wasn't supposed to know anything and Papa was more preoccupied with what I would tell my brother Aziz, who had just come back from England. The most important thing was for me to stick to my story—I was coming back from a lengthy stay in Tunisia with my uncles and aunts.

When we were alone, he gave free rein to his anger and bitterness: "Why did you come back? Why are you here sticking yourself in the lion's maw? Why, Soraya? I was ready to take any risk, ready to die so you could be saved. But here there's nothing I can do to protect you. Nothing, and that makes me crazy! I managed to find you shelter in a free country and you ruined your chance. It's madness to come back to Libya. Madness to expose yourself to the insanities of Bab al-Azizia!"

Very early the next morning we drove to Sirte. We said very little during the four- or five-hour journey. I could see that my father was still angry. We found Mama in her hair salon, where she took me in her arms. "You've lost weight. You've become very beautiful . . ." Stepping back a little, she looked at me, both my hands in hers. "But a little too tanned." I didn't tell her that this new color was because Warda had made me go to a tanning place just before my trip. I know Hicham hadn't liked my new "African" complexion either.

"You work too hard, Mama! You keep on slaving away. Why don't you stop? You look tired."

"What world are you living in, Soraya? How would the family get fed? How would you have received any money in Paris if this salon weren't here?"

In our apartment on Dubai Street I had barely put down my suitcase when Mabrouka's number appeared on my cell phone. It was like being stabbed with a dagger. I ignored the call. But she called back a second time, and then a third. I was terrified, feeling she was in the room with me. And finally I picked up: "Hello?"

"Well, hello there, Princess!"

I didn't answer.

"So how was your little trip to France?"

"Who told you I was in France?"

"You forget that we are the State. Our services know everything about you. Come to your master immediately!"

"I am in Sirte."

"You're lying! We looked for you in Sirte."

"I am there right now."

"Fine. We, too, will be there—next week, with your master. Believe me, he will find you."

A few days later she phoned again. "Where are you?"

"In my mother's hair salon."

"I'm coming."

I'd been tracked down. There was just time enough to say a word or two to Mama, who was dismayed. She called again: "I am here. Come out right now!"

Her car was parked in front of the salon, the back door open. I got in. The driver took off at flying speed. The nightmare was beginning all over again. I knew where we were going. I could guess what was awaiting me. But what else could I have done if I didn't want my whole family to suffer because of me?

Salma received me with a contemptuous smile and Fatiha grabbed my arm: "Quick, to the lab. We need a complete analysis." I didn't resist, didn't protest; my urge to live had been obliterated. I'd become like a robot. They made me wait two or three hours, and then Salma snarled: "Go upstairs to your master!" He was wearing a red tracksuit, his hair was tangled, and his look was satanic. He growled: "Come here, you whore."

I spent the rest of the night in what had been my temporary room once before, next to Farida. I was bruised all over, bleeding, and filled with hatred. I hated myself for having come back to Libya. I really regretted not having succeeded in building a life in France. I hadn't known how to handle myself, how to find the right people, how to land a job. It was as if from the very first day on the Champs-Elysées they had taken me for a loose woman, just an object, a whore, as Gaddafi said. As if that label were glued on my forehead. Farida began to snigger and to be deliberately annoying. "I know other girls who went abroad to be whores," she said. "So pathetic! No honor, no loyalty, no values, no backbone. Guttersnipes who come back to see Papa with their tail between their legs."

I lost it. I jumped on her, hit and shook her furiously. I felt an absolute rage I'd never experienced before. I had no control over myself; I was boiling inside. Mabrouka emerged and tried to separate us, but I was like a lioness that won't let go of its prey. I was holding on to Farida, who was crying with fear, when Mabrouka raised her voice and tried to remove me. I screamed: "Oh, you, just shut up!" It petrified her. No one had ever spoken to her like that. All the girls fell in line in front of the great mistress. Salma came running and slapped me hard across the face; the mark was visible for a long time afterward. "Who do you think you are to take that tone with Mabrouka?" I thought she'd twisted my head off.

They led me through a maze of unfamiliar hallways to a tiny, dark, disgusting room, without a window or air conditioner, although it was almost a hundred degrees. A musty smell almost suffocated me and there were cockroaches. I sobbed, tore my hair out until I had no strength left, and then collapsed on the straw mattress.

A few hours later Fatiha opened the door: "Your master wants you." I went upstairs to find Farida nestled against the Guide, with her head on his torso, which she was caressing and kissing. She moaned: "Soraya is mean and she's crazy. If you had only seen, Master, how she hit me!" Directing his gaze at me, he said to her: "Go ahead, whore. You may give her a smack back." She leaped at me and gave me two. "Let go! I told you one only!" He dismissed her with his madman's eyes and turned to me: "Ah, I like that! You are a wild beast. Oh, I really like that, that fury inside you! That passion!" He ripped off my clothes and threw me on the bed.

"I beg you! Don't do anything to me, I'm in too much pain! I beg you!"

"She's fighting back, the tigress! I like this new temperament. So it was France, eh, that gave you this rage!"

Since I was bleeding profusely, he took the red towel to catch the blood: "This is good. Oh, this is really good!" "Stop," I screamed. "Please, I beg of you! I am in too much pain!" He pulled me to the shower and urinated on me. I was hollering in agony. He rang the bell and a Ukrainian nurse came in. Claudia. A busty redhead with the face of an angel. She took me to the laboratory and gave me painkillers and a soothing lotion. Her gestures were unerring; she was used to this part of the job. I wanted to go back to my room but had to turn around to avoid a large delegation of Africans who had come to meet with the Guide in his tent.

The next day everyone was supposed to leave for Tripoli. I planted myself in front of Mabrouka, knowing something was broken deep inside of me. I felt hard and rigid now.

"I'm staying. I am sick. Going with you is out of the question."

"You've become hardheaded, arrogant, and intolerable. You're not worth anything anymore. Go home to your mother!"

Salma tossed me a thousand dinars, as if to a whore after her work is done. "Get the hell out! The driver is waiting!"

I dashed into the car. My phone showed about a dozen calls from Hicham. And a message: "If you don't answer it's because you're with the other one. He will always triumph. I have no desire whatsoever to have such a squalid affair. I'd rather break it off." I opened the window and threw out my cell phone.

They dropped me off at home and I found my mother there. She, too, had tried to reach me and seemed at the end of her rope.

"I have to change my life, Mama," I told her. "I have to start from scratch. Bab al-Azizia, Hicham—that's all over and done with."

"Hicham? You saw that guy again? You lied to me again?"

"Mama! That 'guy' is the one who gave me the strength to survive. I will never forget that."

Mama gave me a disgusted look. As if suddenly I was the guilty one and not the victim any longer. As if Hicham and Gaddafi belonged to the same perverted universe. It was unbearable.

The atmosphere at home was becoming heavily charged. My mere presence exasperated my mother. No longer was I her daughter—I was a woman who'd been touched by men and lost all her value. Her looks, her sighs, her thoughts—everything screamed of my guilt in her eyes. But she kept herself from stating what was on her mind, until one day she let all her resentment explode: "I can't take it anymore. We have no life this way. Your father and I don't deserve this. Nor do your brothers! The whole family has become a target of ridicule for the neighborhood."

"Who are you talking about? If people know anything it's because you told them!"

"They're not stupid, Soraya! Everyone has noticed the merry-go-round—your disappearance, the dance of cars from Bab al-Azizia. What a disgrace! We used to be a respectable family but now we have to hug the walls. It's too much to bear—such a waste!"

I preferred the idea of going back to Tripoli with Papa. The city was bigger and I'd feel a little less stifled. Hicham tried to get in touch again. He turned up in front of the house, honked his horn, then called me, putting his hands around his mouth like a loudspeaker. I was afraid of the neighbors' reactions and preferred calling him from my new phone. But what was the point in seeing him? Why risk exposing him to the wrath of Gaddafi and his henchmen? I knew they were perfectly capable of killing for less than what he'd done.

When Mama came to Tripoli for Friday, the day of prayer, in confidence I gently hinted at a problem I was having with my chest. Because they had been pushed, crushed, and bitten, my breasts were drooping and very painful. I was twenty-one years old and had the chest of an old lady. It threw her into a spin. I had to see a doctor, of course. Find a specialist. In Tunisia, of course. She gave me four thousand dinars and arranged for me to travel to Tunis with my little brother. A respectable young woman never travels alone, after all.

When I came home, another ordeal was awaiting me: Aziz was about to get married to a young girl from Sirte. I should have been happy—wedding celebrations are joyful occasions, where new encounters can take place. Every girl my age loves them. You get dressed up, have your hair done, put on makeup. You meet a cousin for the first time . . . it's a place to be seen . . . But that was just it: how could I not dread the looks, questions, rumors that my absence must have aroused at previous family gatherings? I was growing anxious. And then, I was jealous as well, why not just admit it? The young bride would be a virgin, beautiful and respected, whereas I felt completely dried up.

At the wedding, I acted restrained, tried not to be noticed. Mama was appalled that I didn't want to wear a long dress. I preferred a pretty colored shirt over a pair of elegant black jeans. I served everyone unobtrusively and had my answers ready for the inevitable questions: I'd been in school in Tripoli, then to the university to study dentistry. Yes, everything was fine. Would I get married? One day, of course . . . "I have a husband for you," some of the aunts then whispered. It made me smile. I had saved the day.

In Tripoli life went back to its routine. Aziz came back to live there with his wife. They took the large bedroom and I had to pretend to be a little girl again. All the more so because my brother began to play the role of head of the family, horrified by my cigarettes—which I smoked only in the bathroom anyway—and often ready to hit me. I didn't recognize him. And he must have felt the same way. On several occasions a driver from Bab al-Azizia came to pick me up, but he left without me. They said I wasn't there. I was surprised that they weren't more persistent.

Then I made the mistake that destroyed my mother's trust in me once and for all. I used Bab al-Azizia as a cover for slipping away with Hicham for a few days at the end of the year 2010. Really ironic, isn't it? I used a phone call from Mabrouka as an excuse and said to my mother: "I'll probably be three or four days." It was abhorrent, but I had no other way to grab a little bit of freedom.

When I came home, war was declared. Bab al-Azizia had asked for me while I was away. In the eyes of my family I was truly a lost cause this time.

11

LIBERATION

On February 15, the population of Benghazi went out into the streets. It was a crowd of women. Mothers, sisters, wives of political prisoners who'd been assassinated in 1996 in the Abu Salim prison while protesting the sudden incarceration of their lawyer. The news stunned everyone, although I knew that many people in Tripoli were preparing to demonstrate two days later, on February 17, decreed the "day of anger." This impulse of exasperation and revolt I began to sense in the people was fascinating. I had no idea what it might all lead to. Muammar seemed eternal to me, someone who could never be ousted. But in astonishment I noticed more and more demonstrations of disrespect against him. Mockery and sarcasm. People continued to be afraid, aware of the fact that he had the life and death of every Libyan in his hands. But that fear was tinged with scorn and hatred. And the people of Tripoli were expressing it more and more openly.

On February 16, driven perhaps by the budding revolution, I left the house. It was my small personal revolution. Were they seeing me as a slut? So be it. I would add some grist to their mill. I had left my family to go live with Hicham, a young man who was not my husband, something not only inconceivable but illegal in Libya, where any sexual relationship outside of marriage is strictly forbidden. But what should the law matter to me after all the violations I had seen, perpetrated by the very person who ought to personify that law? Did they dare condemn me for wanting to live with the man I loved, when the master of Libya had imprisoned and raped me for years on end?

Hicham and I moved into a little bungalow he had built himself in Enzara, in the suburbs of Tripoli. He was working for a fisherman, diving to catch octopus. I would wait for him and prepare the food. I didn't ask for anything else. I would like to have attended the big demonstration of February 17, but that was impossible; I was too far away. And so I stayed glued to the television, where Al Jazeera was broadcasting the images of the rebellion live. I was thrilled! What a movement! What nerve! The Libyans were rebelling, Libya was waking up. Finally! I erased every number of Bab al-Azizia from my telephone. From now on they had greater emergencies to deal with than trying to find me.

And then one day, Al Jazeera showed a young woman, Inas Al-Obeidi, storming into the dining room of a luxury hotel in

Tripoli where the Western press was staying, screaming that she had been raped by Gaddafi's militia. It was an incredible scene. You could see her shout out her story as security or protocol men rushed forward to silence her. But she kept going—weeping, fighting. Journalists were trying to intervene, but in the end she was carried away forcibly, leaving the entire world speechless. Her courage astounded me. Surely, they would call her a madwoman. Or a prostitute. But she was lifting the veil from the case of thousands of women, for I didn't doubt for a second that Gaddafi's troops committed rape, emulating their master.

Then some friends of Hicham passed him the message that Bab al-Azizia, now on its guard, wanted to eliminate those "girls" who had become troublesome and beyond redemption. I learned that some armed men, paid by Gaddafi—the famous Kataebs—had come looking for me at home and had threatened my parents. Terrified, Mama had taken refuge in Morocco. Interrogated harshly, Papa had said that I had followed her. "Make her come home!" he'd been ordered. Some Kataebs had also gone to the house of Hicham's parents and asked where I was. The family had answered that they didn't know me, but Hicham was summoned to the police station there. "I need to take you to Tunisia," he told me. "There's not a moment to lose."

He entrusted me to a friend who drove an ambulance and I crossed the border to meet up with my Tunisian cousins. I followed the news from Libya every single day. The NATO strikes, the advances the rebels were making, the savagery of the front lines. I was living in constant anguish and wanted to go back to Libya, but Hicham staunchly refused. He was afraid that the rebels would think me an accessory of the Gaddafi clique, a member of his first circle, would assume I was corrupt, had no dignity. The thought seemed insane to me! Me, an accomplice? Me, who had been kidnapped and enslaved? Me, who, in order to set my life's path right, had no other hope than to see Gaddafi destitute and finally judged for what he had done to me? I yelled into the phone that his fears were ridiculous and even insulting. That it was the last straw for them to say I was in league with the people who had tortured me! Then I heard rumors that Najah and Farida had been killed. And suddenly I was frightened.

In August, as Ramadan began, I heard that a clairvoyant had predicted Gaddafi's death and the liberation of Tripoli for February 20. So I went back home, first going to Hicham at his little bungalow. But the situation there was unbearable—there was no water, no gas, no electricity, no gasoline. The NATO strikes continued; it was total chaos. On August 8 a group of Gaddafi supporters came to ask Hicham and his brother to participate in a nighttime operation near Zawiya. I believe it had something to do with the evacuation of a family by boat, but I have to admit that I didn't get all the details. Perhaps he didn't want to upset me. He seemed distressed and I had the feeling that he had no choice. One evening he left and never came back.

Soon afterward I got a phone call telling me that a NATO strike had hit their boat. Shaken by the news, I rushed to Hicham's mother's house. She was crying and took me in her arms, although God knows she had always disapproved of our relationship. I inundated her with questions but she knew very little more than I did. The information was contradictory and patchy. All they knew was that Hicham was thought to be dead. His brother had swum for nine hours to get back to shore and was safe, though he had leg injuries. But he couldn't tell us what had happened. Hicham was missing and probably dead, even though his body wasn't found, unlike the others'. A funeral service was held. I was devastated.

Then came August 23 and the liberation of Tripoli. The people were in the street—numb, euphoric, and relieved all at the same time. Women came out with their children, displaying the colors of our new flag. Men were embracing, dancing, firing off bursts with their Kalashnikovs toward the sky and shouting "Allahu Akbar." Loudspeakers everywhere were broadcasting revolutionary songs and the rebels, exhausted and happy, were welcomed as true heroes. They had opened up the prisons and besieged Bab al-Azizia! It was unimaginable. I ululated, applauded the convoys, thanked God for what would always be the greatest day in Libya's history. But inside I was weeping. I was washed out and lost. Hicham wasn't there to see this day with me.

All night long and over the next few days, the television aired fascinating images of rebel troops entering the citadel, searching the houses and villas of the Gaddafi clan, sporting objects that belonged to the Guide like so many outlandish trophies. They derided his bad taste and the ridiculous opulence of his sons' properties. His busts and photographs were disfigured, stomped on, ripped apart. Safia's house was presented as the "family home" in which the Guide's bedroom presumably adjoined that of his wife. I shrugged my shoulders. Clearly, nobody had the slightest idea of what schemes went on behind the secured gates of Bab al-Azizia. Nobody would ever be able to imagine that a handful of poor wretches had been living in its basements.

At the time, I was being housed temporarily by the girlfriend of one of Hicham's buddies, but Papa was worried for me. On August 28, when he told me that my brother's newborn child needed urgent treatment in Tunisia, I asked to leave with them. I returned to Tripoli in late September.

But what to do with my life? How to get any control over it? I was only twenty-two but had the strange feeling that I'd already seen too much, lived through too much, had weary eyes and a spent body. That I was depleted forever. No resilience, no desires, no hope. My life was a dead end. I had no money, no education, no profession. Living with my family had become impossible—my brothers knew the truth. So where to live? No Libyan hotel is allowed to let an unaccompanied woman have a room. No respectable landlord will rent a room to an unmarried woman. Hayat, my sweet Tunisian cousin, had accepted my request to come with me to Tripoli for a while, but then what?

I'd heard that the International Criminal Court had ordered a warrant for the arrest of Gaddafi for crimes against humanity. So then I put all my hopes on the strength of my testimony. I had to be heard. I had to tell my story and draw up a merciless indictment against my torturer myself. For I wanted to see him behind bars. I wanted to confront him in a last face-to-face—look him straight in the eye and ask him coldly: "Why? Why did you do that to me? Why did you rape me? Why did you incarcerate me, beat me, drug me, insult me? Why did you teach me to drink and smoke? Why did you rob me of my life? Why?"

And then he was dead, executed on October 20 by the rebels, having barely made it out of a sewer where he was hiding. How ironic for the person who had treated his people like rats! I saw his bloodied face and his body displayed in a cold storage room in Misrata, like a piece of damaged meat. I don't know what I felt most strongly—the relief of knowing him to be defeated once and for all, the terror of seeing all that violence, or the anger of seeing him get away from any sort of judgment. It must have been the anger, I'm sure. Gaddafi died without having to account to the Libyan people he had trampled on for forty-two years, without appearing before any international court, without having to answer before the entire world. And, above all, before me.

Some of the rebels, to whom I told my story, took me to the former Military Academy for Women, where one of their brigades is now located. They questioned me for a long time, promising me justice. They told me: "There are lots of girls in the same position as you." They assigned me temporary housing, former apartments of Gaddafi's mercenaries. Mistakenly, I felt safe there. But a rebel abused me sexually. A girl with a past like mine . . .

This time I brought charges. In spite of excoriation and threats, I stuck to my guns. Libya today thinks of itself as a state of law, and I try to have faith. But I had to move. And hide. And attempt to ignore the insults on my cell phone, whose violence increased twofold.

There you have it. I think I've told you everything. For me, this was something I had to do, maybe even my duty. Believe me, it wasn't easy. I still have to do battle with an overload of feelings that are clattering away inside my brain and won't give me any peace. Fear, shame, sadness, bitterness, disgust, rebellion. What a combination of emotions! Some days these feelings coalesce into a strength that brings me back a little confidence in my future. But more often they overwhelm me, push me into a well of sadness from which I don't feel I can emerge. A lost girl, my parents sigh. A girl who doesn't deserve to live, according to my brothers, whose honor is at stake. And that thought chills my bones. Cutting my throat would make respected men of them. Crime would wash away shame. I am defiled, so I defile others. I'm a deadbeat, so who would cry over my death?

I would like to make a life in the new Libya, but I wonder if that's possible.

PART TWO
THE INVESTIGATION

1

IN SORAYA'S FOOTSTEPS

Soraya doesn't make things up. She recounts what she has seen, experienced, felt, without hesitating to recognize what she doesn't know, doesn't understand, or is unfamiliar with. There's no desire to exaggerate the story or expand her role in it. She never extrapolates or makes guesses. Frequently, when I asked her for details, she'd say: "Sorry, I know nothing about that. I wasn't there." She doesn't wish to be credible, she wants to be believed. And within that demand lies something crucial. Besides, those were the terms of our agreement: better some silence than an approximation. The slightest misrepresentation would ruin the credibility of the whole testimony. So she told it all, even correcting her father when he wanted to play with the facts a bit. At times, when she described scenes with Gaddafi, she would apologize for using crude words, which she deemed degrading for a woman. But what else could she do? On the other hand, it amused her to think about the problems of translating her Arabic to my French: "I really wonder what word you're going to use there! I'm not making your task any easier, am I?"

What a wonderful storyteller! She took part in the interview very willingly and with a courage that touched me. We met every day, early in the year 2012, in the apartment in Tripoli where she was temporarily living, as well as (though less often) in my hotel room. She'd dive into her account passionately, immersing herself in the situations, miming the scenes like a series of skits as she reconstructed the dialogues, waving her hands, raising her voice and her eyebrows, sometimes getting up to play all the characters, from Gaddafi to Mabrouka, or even Tony Blair.

I will never forget what it felt like to watch her relive certain crucial moments of her life, the horror of which hasn't left her, nor the distress I felt hearing the despair in her voice at times. Nor will I ever forget the anxiety I felt for her future, or how we would laugh together, madly, when at the end of a long conversation she'd turn on the television to a channel with Egyptian videos, tie a scarf with metallic sequins around her hips, and—sexy and irresistible—would try to teach me how to belly dance. "Stand up straight, Annick! Arms wide, chest forward, big smile! That's right! Sway and roll your hips!"

After Gaddafi's death, Soraya's relationship with her family continued to get worse, which isolated her even further. So she didn't want me to see her parents before leaving Tripoli. Fortunately, I had already met her father in January 2012. A small man with stooped shoulders, balding head, and a look of despondency. One evening, almost on the sly, without having told his wife, he came to visit his daughter and was watching her with infinite affection.

"She's the one," he told me, "who used to create the atmosphere in our home ever since she was very little. She was a born comedian! From the day she disappeared the house sank into a sadness from which it has never emerged." He was angry with himself for not having been in Sirte the day the Colonel visited his daughter's school. "If you only knew how I've imagined the scene of the bouquet of flowers and replayed it in my head—hundreds of times! I'm sure that some of Gaddafi's people had already gone to the hair salon to take a look at Soraya. And I suspect that the principal of the school was in cahoots with the Gaddafi clique to line up a band of girls that would definitely please him. Then all that was needed was any old pretext for introducing them to him. I now am certain that Gaddafi had a gang of criminals in every region of Libya do this dirty work."

He was still furiously stewing over what had happened and shaking his head, lost in his thoughts, his regrets, and his remorse. "If I'd been there I would never have let Soraya leave with those three women under such a stupid pretext! It made no sense whatsoever! When my wife alerted me, without daring to say too much over the phone—all of Libya knew the phones were bugged—I rushed from Tripoli to Sirte and shouted at her for what she'd done, insofar as is permissible. We didn't sleep for one night, two nights, three nights, and I felt like I was going mad. I wanted the earth to swallow me up. Soraya's friends, her teachers, our neighbors, the customers at the hair salon, everyone kept asking: 'Where is she?' Then I went back to Tripoli so her mother could tell the story that she was there with her Papa."

And the idea of making an official complaint? To whom? Why? Soraya had left in an official car, surrounded by bodyguards who worked for the Guide. Any protest was unthinkable. "Who would dream of bringing charges against the devil when you are in hell?" And when her parents received confirmation that their worst fear was true and that Gaddafi had very much made Soraya his prey, they were distraught. "The choice was obvious: dishonor or death. Criticizing, protesting, or complaining was equal to a death sentence. So I holed up in Tripoli and lost the taste of happiness forever."

He so wanted justice to be done to his daughter, so she could come back with her head held high, her "honor cleansed" before the whole extended family. But that was impossible, as he knew. "Everyone around us doubts Soraya's story and sees me as almost 'subhuman,' and I can see why—there is no shame more dreadful than what Gaddafi did to us. It affects my sons as well. They are shadows of their former selves, so self-conscious they are, incapable of thinking of any way to look like real men other than killing their sister. It's horrible!

Soraya has no chances whatsoever in Libya anymore. Our society is too stupid, too traditional, and too unforgiving. You know what? As painful as it would be for me as her father, I wish a family abroad would adopt her."

I felt I had to go to Sirte, Gaddafi's city. I wanted to see the building where Soraya had grown up, the hair salon that her mother had kept going so single-mindedly, the school where the scene with the bouquet of flowers had taken place. Soraya wasn't enthusiastic and refused to come with me, but she understood why I needed to go. She herself was wondering what was happening to the city, a Gaddafi stronghold located 360 kilometers from Tripoli, once just a small fishing village, but a place the ruler of Libya had dreamed of transforming into the capital of the United States of Africa. Instead, in the fall of 2011, it had become the location of a tough and bloody siege, as it underwent bombing by NATO. From then on people would talk about it as a ghost town, eroded by resentment and sick with its now destroyed dreams of grandeur. Having decided to take refuge there in the final hour, thereby bringing a deluge of steel, gunpowder, and fire down upon it, Gaddafi had certainly not done it any favors.

The road to Sirte was long, straight, and terribly monotonous. It cut through huge desertlike expanses where herds of sheep and a few intermittent grayish camels stood out against a metallic sky. Every now and again some rain would fall, washing the windshield. Then the wind would pick up, raising whirlwinds of sand, which made driving quite treacherous. Silhouettes of Bedouins standing by the side of the road, one hand holding the protective scarf over their faces, would suddenly materialize through the sand, and we worried that animals could emerge out of the dust at any moment. At the checkpoints, hooded rebels with sunglasses to shield their eyes from the sand motioned for people to pass with a simple gesture of their Kalashnikov, not concerned with checking people's papers. It was terrible weather for a visit—people say that the desert wind makes people crazy. Thankfully the sun eventually began to break through and Sirte, or rather its skeleton, appeared.

I saw lines of empty, devastated, looted homes, shells of buildings, their walls blackened, with bullet holes from the rockets and mortars. A few houses and other structures in ruins. There, the battles had been desperate and fierce. A little farther on the fighting had been less serious. Although it was rare to see undamaged buildings, a few shops here and there along the wide palm-lined avenues were open. "Life picked up quickly," one merchant told me. "Some people fled, of course, and they won't be seen again. But now seventy percent of the seventy thousand inhabitants have come back. And they are adapting and rebuilding. They might as well pile up with ten other people in the only room of their home that's closed to the outside. What else can you do?"

The section of Dubai Street where Soraya's family apartment stood was relatively well preserved. The three- and four-story white buildings, lined up and identical, showed few scars. Porches had been repainted in green (Gaddafi's color had been banned throughout the country, but perhaps they needed to use up some old supplies of paint) and under the arcades some of the clothing stores, drugstores, and cosmetics shops were open. The hair salon was on a side street, pierced with bullet holes; the metal roller window was drawn, which could have been misleading. But a neighbor showed me that it served to protect the customers from the looks of passersby, since the window was broken and couldn't be replaced. Inside, an employee was applying golden streaks to the hair of a young sophisticated-looking patron; another one came up to me with a smile, explaining that the appointment book was filled up for the rest of the day. Three women in skintight jeans, veils over their hair, were waiting and staring at me. I was told that the owner wasn't here at this time. I glanced around, trying to catch some detail that would remind me of Soraya, but there were no photographs or any other decorations on the black and pink walls. Just oval mirrors in which I would have liked to have seen her reflection.

Impatient, I charged over to Soraya's school. "The School of the Revolution." It was an immense building, sand-colored and white, which seemed to have survived the bombing intact or else had been well restored. It was a little past one o'clock and dozens of children—girls and boys—were jostling each other in the hallways. Vast freshly painted staircases echoed with their voices. Outside, other students were scattered in an interior courtyard paved with pink slabs that led to a gymnasium and an athletic field. The girls were wearing the very uniform that Soraya had described—black pants and tunic, a white scarf covering their hair—but their young age took me by surprise. Soraya had described a school that accepted only the three years of the *lycée,* which means students between fifteen and seventeen. Was I in the right place?

A man with an emaciated face and a thick mustache reassured me. NATO had bombed two schools in Sirte where ammunition had been stored, which were completely destroyed. Thus they had to organize it so that the students could be on rotating schedules to take maximum advantage of the buildings that were left standing. The buildings housed one school in the morning, another in the afternoon. A staff member called the principal of the girls' *lycée* on his cell phone; he had already left, as his school met in the morning. He arrived a few minutes later. Tall, athletic, his face framed by a heavy beard. Aloof and anxious. We settled down in an empty classroom and he explained the flood of difficulties he'd had to face so that his 913 students could come back on January 15, two weeks later than the rest of Libya. Quite a feat, given the fact that the fighting here had lasted a lot longer than elsewhere. The parents had been mobilized, and everyone had pitched in to clear away the rubble, reconstruct doors, windows, and bathrooms, and repaint the whole building. All the equipment—microscopes, televisions, computers—had been stolen; the school's offices, libraries, and laboratories had been totally looted.

For lack of any help from the state the families had pooled together. Sirte was hurting, drained, but that was no reason for the children's education to suffer. Everything was already hard enough. "No one has any idea how traumatized our students are! Some families lost as many as five of their family members during the final battles. Occasionally some of the girls suddenly become hysterical in class or black out. One word, one image can unleash waterfalls of tears. Our one and only social worker is no longer enough—we now need psychiatrists."

The school didn't have enough teachers. Some of the female instructors had lost their husbands in the battle of Sirte and weren't able—or didn't want—to come back to teach. A section of the staff had vanished. Dead? "No, they just left," the principal said soberly. Like the former principal. "He left Libya. We've had no word from him." He was most likely too much of a Gaddafi supporter to hope to survive his hero without any problems. So this man, Mohammed Ali Moufta, had been nominated to succeed him. He had been teaching at the school for nineteen years and felt he was up to assuming his new responsibilities. All the more so, he assured me, because, contrary to the rumor, there would be no "shake-up" in the educational curriculum.

I was startled. Hadn't the new minister of education just confirmed the urgency of a pedagogical upheaval, the necessary overhaul of every program, and the creation of a team of

experts responsible for rewriting the school manuals in their
entirety? Some of the rebels had, in my presence, mentioned
some of the educational aberrations Gaddafi had conceived.
For example, the geography courses introduced the Arab
world as an indivisible entity and maps showed only the names
of cities, without ever drawing the borders of the individual
countries. The study of the *Green Book* used to take up several
hours a week and be spread out over many years. The teaching of Western languages such as English and French had been
banned in the early eighties in favor of sub-Saharan languages
such as Swahili and Hausa. As for Libyan history, it quite
simply began with the Guide—the kingdom of the Sanussi
before 1969 wasn't even mentioned. "Our school is primarily
one of science," the principal said drily, "so we aren't terribly
concerned with the changes, especially since we are already
experimenting with a teaching method from Singapore. As for
courses in political culture, we simply did away with them."

That is when I asked my question, the one that had obsessed
me since my arrival within the walls of this school. April 2004.
Colonel Gaddafi's visit. The presentation of bouquets and gifts
by a few pretty female students. And the abduction of one of
them, spotted by Gaddafi, a girl who would become his sexual
slave. Had he heard the story? Flames lit up in his charcoal
black eyes. I had barely finished my sentence when he yelled:
"That's untrue! Outrageous! Idiotic!" Excuse me? "Your story
makes no sense! Colonel Gaddafi never visited any schools!"
He was aghast, beside himself. I continued in a calm voice: "I

have met with the girl. Her testimony is serious. She has given me all the details." "It's false, I tell you! Completely false!" It was becoming frightening to hear how he raised his voice. I went on: all of Libya was accustomed to seeing the Guide visit schools and universities, even in the middle of the revolution; newspapers published photographs, the TV showed films of him . . . "Not in Sirte! That was HIS city! We've been blamed enough for that already. He never came to any school in Sirte! I guarantee it!" At that point I would have liked it so much if Soraya had been with me, so she could have crushed him with the details of her testimony. Three days later, when I reported the whole scene to her, and showed her pictures of the school, she was overcome, before exploding in a rage.

I persisted. The Guide had children of cousins and other members of his tribe in this school. Being familiar with his interest in education, whose codes he dictated, it wasn't all that absurd that he would pay a friendly visit, was it? Mohammed Ali Moufta didn't yield. "Never! That's just malicious gossip! It may have occurred that he addressed the students via a video that we projected on a big screen. But that's all!" Insisting was pointless; I wouldn't get any further. And suddenly it seemed dangerous to give Soraya's name—which, strangely, he hadn't asked for—as it might have exposed her family to some retaliation. Sirte had plainly not turned the page.

I was about to leave the place when I suddenly noticed a bunch of very young female teachers in a small room that opened out onto the wide landing of the second floor. They were coming and going, undoubtedly between two classes, to have some tea, put down a bag, and laugh with their colleagues. I wormed my way in. They soon huddled around me, offered me a chair and some fruit juice, and within seconds after they closed the door the cubbyhole, full of revolutionary insignia, turned into an aviary. They were all talking at once, trying to outdo each other with stories, memories, and indignation. One would begin a tale, would be interrupted by another who'd chime in, and a third one would complete it, crying: "Wait! I've got something much worse!" to catch our attention. I was having a very hard time getting it all down. It was as if a floodgate had opened. You couldn't stop them.

Girls being abducted? "All of Sirte knew it!" Sirte, which loved Gaddafi? One pretty young woman, her eyes encircled in kohl liner beneath a flawless set of eyebrows, tried to explain to me: "He had a hold over the people of his city, his tribe, his family; the school was raising us to worship him; but everyone knew that morally he was a bastard. And whoever says he didn't know it is lying!" Her five colleagues loudly backed her up, "sickened" by what the principal had said to me. "His predecessor fled after having been part of the last group of Gaddafi supporters. Sadly, the new one is of the same ilk!"

"Ours was the same too," one of the teachers from the school that used the building in the afternoon explained, "before we applied officially to the ministry, saying that he kept criticizing the Western intervention in Libya and poisoning young brains." One of the women avowed she had been a student in Soraya's *lycée* and had seen Gaddafi as he "paraded" in the gymnasium. Through the window, she pointed out the building across the courtyard. She didn't remember Soraya, but she was categorical: the Guide had most certainly been in this place. Her neighbor, with a laughing face enveloped in a red veil, had heard him as well, two years earlier, as he gave an interminable speech at the University of Sirte. "When he arrived, the whole area was blocked, courses were interrupted, and it was as if time was suspended."

He would take every opportunity, they assured me, to meet young girls. He used to invite himself to weddings at the last moment. "Most of the hosts were flattered," one of them said. "But my uncles, even though they were part of his family, immediately prevented me from showing my face." He would regularly invite students to come to the Katiba al-Saadi, where he had his residence, for a festival of songs. "I went there two days in a row with school, but then my parents wouldn't let me go back. 'It's the most dangerous place of all,' said my brother. If the order doesn't come from him directly, it will come from his clique, his officers, his guards, from any military person at all. His morals are contagious!" Gaddafi would even pretend to be sick so students would come to comfort him. "I was sixteen, at the avant-garde Lycée de la Pensée, when a teacher announced that Papa Muammar was sick. They chartered a bus to take us to the barracks, where he received us in the tent. He was wearing a white *djellaba* and a small beige cotton cap, and he hugged us one after another. We were very intimidated, but he didn't look sick at all!" Another one remembered being taken to the same katiba by her school to greet Colonel Chadli Bendjedid, the president of Algeria. "Gaddafi constantly needed to be surrounded by young girls. We served as propaganda for him while feeding his obsession."

One of the teachers finally told me how one day a clan from Misrata organized a grand party of official allegiance to the Guide. Perpetually concerned about the support of the various tribes, Gaddafi loved that kind of demonstration. There he noticed a young girl, a friend of the speaker. The next day, guards came for her at the school. The principal refused: this was not the time, she was taking an exam. But that very same evening she was abducted during a wedding celebration she was attending. She disappeared for three days, during which she was raped by Gaddafi. Barely back home, she was married off to one of his bodyguards. "It was her father, a teacher, who told me this himself, begging me to be careful."

The bell for their classes had already rung and the teachers suddenly dashed off, asking that I not publish their names. Nothing in Sirte is simple. So many inhabitants are brooding over the decline of their city—bitter, filled with hate, and pessimistic—convinced that the new power will make them pay for a long time to come for this visceral connection with the man who once was the Guide.

Following in Soraya's footsteps wasn't exactly comfortable; I was afraid of attracting attention to her or her family, awakening the wrath of her brothers, compromising her future in Libya. Her personal story had to remain secret, more than ever before. The only one who proved to be warm and welcoming to Soraya's attempts to flee, to live again, and to escape from her family wrangles was Hayat, her Tunisian cousin and her only loyal confidante now. Unfortunately, meeting any of the girls who had lived with her at Bab al-Azizia was out of the question for me. The first Amal is married and begs to be forgotten. The second, Amal G., is still using sex and alcohol, yearning for her old master, and loathing the thought that Soraya might betray him. One of Bab al-Azizia's drivers and two women who worked in the Department of Protocol recalled only, when we spoke, that they had come across Soraya fleetingly. That was all. There were so few people with access to his sordid basement.

In Paris, Soraya's Tunisian friend Adel gave me some clues to better understand the failure of her stay in France. I met him in a café at the Porte d'Orléans. Stocky, his hair combed back, and with a very gentle face, he spoke to me about Soraya with tenderness and nostalgia. "She arrived broken, uneducated, without the slightest experience in work, schedules, discipline, of life in society. Like a little girl who has totally forgotten what the world is like. Or like a fledgling bird trying to take flight but constantly crashing into the windowpane." He tried to help her as best he could—taking her in when it became obvious that she couldn't stay at Warda's any longer; doing his utmost to find her work, including a brief period at a hairdresser's, cut short because Soraya didn't speak French;

seeing a lawyer so that she could obtain papers; keeping her clothed and fed for several months. "It was terrible to watch her struggle and always fail. Deluded by false promises, abused by men who only wanted to take advantage of her."

Of course, her big mistake was to not start learning French right away. Her early encounters are to blame. She ran into Warda and a few others at La Marquise, the restaurant that specializes in Lebanese food where I went one night and that between midnight and dawn changes into an oriental nightclub. It was so much easier to live in the Arab-speaking world. But that prohibited any integration into French society, any possibility of making connections, of being trained, or of finding employment. True, Soraya didn't try all that hard, incapable as she was of going to bed before four in the morning or getting up before eleven, rebelling against any form of discipline and any orders, no matter who gave them. As if, after Gaddafi, no one could boast of having any right or authority over her ever again.

Having prematurely lost his father in Gabès, Adel, the oldest of three boys, learned early on to play the paterfamilias. He dropped his studies to help his family, then immigrated to France, where he started up a small construction and renovation company in Paris, working extremely hard to build his business. He had welcomed Soraya as if she were "the new baby in the family." She was vulnerable and he needed to take care of her. He was, of course, also a little bit in love with her. Who wouldn't be after watching Soraya dance at La Marquise, swirling her mass of ebony hair and laughing wildly? Too free, too radiant, she irritated the other girls but broke every popularity record among the staff. During the day she'd smoke, talk on the phone, and watch TV. Sometimes she'd cry, racked by memories, questions, apprehensions. It seems that she could tell Adel anything, which included speaking about Gaddafi with what he called "a strange mixture of hatred, rage, and respect." Soraya would balk at this last word, but it is not really surprising that a kind of deference would be mixed in with her rejection of and resentment against the one who was in control of her life and death at such an impressionable age.

"I know she wanted me to devote more time to her," Adel said regretfully, "go out with her during the day and adapt to her nightly rhythm, without any constraint. But I couldn't—I was exhausted! Life in France isn't easy to manage as an immigrant. It requires willpower and a lot of hard work. She didn't understand; she wasn't ready for it." Their living together had to come to an end.

Adel didn't drop her when she got a job, first in one bar and then another. He would visit her in her attic room and bring her groceries. "It was easy to see she wasn't doing well." When she called him to let him know she was flying back to Libya, he couldn't believe it. "You're not really going to do that! You can't!" She called him a few hours later from Tripoli.

"Soraya! You've made a very big mistake."

"I had no choice!"

"Well, you'll have to accept the consequences."

2

"LIBYA," KHADIJA, LEILA . . . AND SO MANY MORE

I would like to be able to tell other stories besides Soraya's. To mention other tragedies lived through by young women who had the misfortune of crossing the path of the "Guide" one day and seeing their lives abruptly and dramatically change. To prove that this was a system that involved countless accomplices and continued for a very long time. But the women are not easy to find.

Many fled Libya when Tripoli was liberated, worried that they would be seen as collaborators with Gaddafi. After all, had they not lived at Bab al-Azizia? Hadn't they also often worn his uniform and enjoyed enormous advantages reserved only for the dictator's clique? Clearly, appearances were against them, and most of them didn't want to run the risk of explaining to the rebels that they never had a choice in what they'd done. So what mercy could they expect—the girls who were known by the Libyans as Gaddafi's "whores," who many thought deserved only to be in prison. Having broken ties with their families a long time ago, many of them are now trying to survive in Tunisia, Egypt, or Beirut, often practicing the only profession they ever learned from the Guide that can bring in any money.

Others had already left for the Libyan countryside before the revolution, frequently getting married, on Gaddafi's orders, to one of his male guards when the Guide himself had grown tired of them; sometimes, though more rarely, they married one of Gaddafi's cousins, to whom they never said anything of what had been done to them, having undergone an operation abroad to reconstruct their hymens. Sometimes they stayed single, a very difficult status in Libya and the source of much suspicion. As sexual relations outside of marriage are forbidden by law, these women risk imprisonment were they to be known to have—or suspected of having—a lover. After imprisonment, women convicted of this crime would be placed in an institute for young offenders under the authority of the state, a place they cannot leave unless their family takes them in or a husband presents himself. Who, then, would dare take the risk of publicly admitting to a sexual relationship with

Gaddafi, even if it *was* forced upon them? It would be tantamount to suicide.

Not to mention the danger of retaliation—by the men in their family, for being dishonored; by rebels and relatives of "martyrs" of the revolution, thirsting for revenge; by Gaddafi supporters by whose side they could have remained at Bab al-Azizia and who, with good reason, dread their testimonies.

In April 2011, one woman came forward, just one, right in the middle of the fighting. Solemnly and of her own accord, the former Gaddafi bodyguard, fifty-two years old, appeared on television in Benghazi. Wearing large sunglasses and wrapped in the revolutionary flag, she expressed the misfortune of those women who, like herself, had made the mistake of joining the revolutionary troops in the seventies, believing in the Guide's sincerity, and who had then been raped and disparaged by him for years on end. More than speaking, she was yelling at the camera full-screen, begging the pro-Gaddafi people to finally open their eyes and calling on the Libyans, the Arabs, and the entire world to avenge the many women who had been violated. This television appearance had stunned the public. For the first time, someone was showing a glimpse of the reality of the life of the "Amazons." Someone had uttered the word "rape" and pointed the finger directly at the dictator himself. "No more pretending now!" she told the regime. "Enough hypocrisy! Wake up, people of Libya!" And then she disappeared.

I wasn't able to contact her until April 2012, a year later. She was still as combative as she'd seemed on the video, and told me a little about her ruined life. The death threats she had received after her television appearance had forced her to flee to Egypt, where she had communicated all the information she had to the Libyan insurgents and to NATO. Someone had made an attempt on her life, but it seemed that nothing could stop her anymore. She had asked to go to the front, had taken up arms in Sirte, and was involved in combat until the very last battle. "That's where I felt most protected."

Fighting didn't make her a heroine. Far from it. The scandal of her televised admissions had provoked an earthquake inside her family; her brothers, tainted with shame and dishonor, had been forced to sell their house and move. She herself was the target of death threats. She had just received another message: "Your name is on the blacklist. We will murder you soon. Allah, Muammar, Libya."

A handful of other terrified women also agreed to confide in me. Some of them I met personally, mostly very briefly. Others, confessing they were incapable of meeting a foreigner eye to eye to reveal their story—a story they had never told before, even to those they were close to—agreed to tell it to a Libyan woman who supported my project, giving her explicit permission to tell it to me. They were convinced of the importance of such a project, but spoke only on the condition that their names would never be mentioned and that I would not provide a single detail that might identify them. "I would kill myself instantly," one woman said, "if I knew that my husband or children could find out about my past one day." I know this woman was not speaking idly.

Here, then, are their stories, as they were told to me, without any connection between them or any transition. This is the raw material that, sadly, no court of justice will ever hear.

LIBYA

The woman who had appeared on television suggests that I call her "Libya" in this book. Of course, that's not her real name. But revealing it would be a death sentence for her, and by using this name she means to express the hope she places in a country finally freed from Gaddafi's yoke. She spent roughly thirty years with the dictator. "A lifetime!" she says soberly. "My life. Ruined." She was at the *lycée* in Benghazi when some young soldiers only slightly older than she recruited her to join a revolutionary committee. This was in the late seventies, when Colonel Gaddafi's *Green Book* had just been published. He'd insisted in its third part on the role and rights of women in Libyan society, calling upon them in the book and in speeches and other propaganda to "liberate themselves from their chains." They must all, he said, serve the revolution and become the finest allies of its leader.

Being drafted into a revolutionary committee was presented as a privilege, a ticket into the country's elite, and so Libya was flattered, even though her parents were somewhat concerned. In any case, they didn't really have any choice: "Refusing would have put them straight in prison." There were many meetings, lofty speeches. Gaddafi occasionally appeared and boosted the morale of the girls, who were prepared to do anything to serve the man who addressed them like a prophet. The tenth anniversary of his revolution was approaching and he wanted to make it a grand event, to be attended in Benghazi by many heads of state. The women in arms would show themselves to be the spearheads of the finest revolution ever.

Libya dropped out of school, became deeply involved in the committee, trained to march in step, and learned how to launch rockets. Gaddafi was right, she thought, to target the women and teach them how to break taboos, even if it meant angering their parents. To hell with the straitjackets of tradition! Freedom was at stake! She was thrilled to be living with her friends at the training center and not at home with her family anymore. On the evening of September 1, 1979, when a great parade was aired on every television channel, they were alerted to the fact that the Colonel wished to greet them in person. And so about ten delighted girls went to his residence, where he was bewitching and charming, before withdrawing to his apartment. The women activists with Gaddafi's small group then asked one of the girls, fifteen years old, to join him there. They dressed her in traditional costume and gave her a thousand recommendations on how to flatter him and glorify his revolution. The girl joyfully entered his apartment.

She came out drained, blood between her thighs. The group of young activists was in a state of shock.

Life went on as before. Libya returned to her family but was less diligent in school and—more and more nervous—attended committee meetings, prodded by very active militant women at the university, who had all passed through the bed of the Guide. As the months went by, her young friends were called in one by one to join Gaddafi in Tripoli, Sirte, or Misrata. A car came to pick them up right where they were, sometimes even a plane. And what they told Libya upon their return drove her to despair. But what could she say? How could she flee?

Her turn came six months after the September 1 festivities, when Gaddafi visited Benghazi. One night, some of the activist women came to collect her and brought her to his residence, undressed her completely, and pushed her into his room despite her tears and supplications: "My mother will kill me! Please, have mercy!" He was waiting for her in a silk robe, raped her without saying a word, then chased her out with a few smacks on her behind. "Perfect, little girl!" She said nothing to her parents, not a word of protestation to the revolutionary committee, where there were threats every day of throwing into a hole the "saboteurs" who dared criticize the Guide, "friend, protector, and liberator of all women." But she withdrew, grew despondent, worrying her parents, who, thinking she was depressed or in love, decided to marry her off without consulting her. One day, on her way home from school, she discovered that a reception was being organized at her house. There was a crowd of guests, an imam was present, and a marriage contract was put under her nose. "Here. This is where you have to sign."

Finding out that same night that she was no longer a virgin, her outraged husband demanded a divorce. He could have sent her away immediately but showed himself to be "compassionate" and waited two weeks. She felt ashamed, not daring to be seen by anyone, panic-stricken at the thought of going home to her parents.

So she phoned . . . Bab al-Azizia. In encouraging the activists to break with their "reactionary" families, had Gaddafi not always reassured them with the fact that he would be there for them? "Take a plane to Tripoli right away!" she was told. A few women were waiting for her at the airport and introduced her to Bab al-Azizia—that vast "harem," as Libya described it. A band of women, living together in double or single rooms, at the mercy of the Guide and his moods, his fantasies, his slightest demands. The majority of these women had been brought to him through the famous revolutionary committees, had been raped, and had no way out other than entering into his service to avoid tainting their families. At least they were fed, housed, and clothed (in the uniforms of guards). At least they had something resembling status (guardians of the revolution). Where they lived, nothing was forbidden: alcohol, cigarettes, and hashish were consumed in great abundance, something Gaddafi himself encouraged. The schedule of the days and nights was unchanging: "We eat, we sleep, we fuck."

Except when the Guide moved to Sirte or another city and the entire household had to follow. Or when he went abroad, trips on which Libya, to her regret, was never invited. "He was afraid I'd use the chance to escape." Some of the women did, indeed, do just that, were found in Turkey, and were brought back to their country, their heads shaven, accused of treason, and shown on television as brothel prostitutes, whereupon they were executed. The house had daily comings and goings of girls who spent one night and then left again, some voluntarily, others by force. "Gaddafi would urge us to bring him our sisters, our cousins, and even our daughters."

One day in 1994, Libya couldn't stop herself from warning one mother against Gaddafi's intentions concerning her two beautiful young daughters. Incredulous and shocked, the mother opened her heart to the Guide about this, who went mad with rage: Libya had violated the omertà, the conspiracy of silence. The penalty for this violation might be her life, so she fled. She took a military plane to Tobruk, then a car to Egypt, where she was arrested because she had no visa. Libyan opponents managed to get her to Iraq, where she spent two weeks, living in fear of the Baa'th Party, then quickly moved on to Greece. Gaddafi's network found her there and, once back in Libya, she was imprisoned for a year and a half in a jail in the basement of a farm before being sent back to . . . Bab al-Azizia, until the beginning of the 2011 revolution. "An old slave woman side by side with the youngest of them," she says. Definitively trapped.

KHADIJA

Khadija is a solemn, disillusioned young woman who, after having been threatened and attacked several times, is aware that her experience and her knowledge of the Gaddafi system puts her in great danger even today, after the fall of his regime. The first time I saw her, early one January morning in 2012, her white tracksuit was covered in blood. As a "warning," some unknown men had abducted and raped her during the night. With attractively curled lips and a slightly hooked nose, she was chain-smoking, biting her nails, and speaking with detachment, if not a certain cynicism. At twenty-seven she admitted to having no illusions whatsoever about anything that the new Libya might have to offer her. She was simply trying to survive somewhere in Tripoli. Her destiny had derailed the day she met Gaddafi, and his death did not allow her to hope for redemption.

In the early years of 2000, Khadija was a first-year law student at the University of Tripoli when an altercation with a school principal caused her to be expelled. Highly upset and at loose ends, she went to the hairdresser and in the salon's protective space recounted her unfortunate experience. One of the customers listened attentively and compassionately. "What's happening to you is just too unfair. But I know someone who can work this out for you: the Guide." Khadija was astounded. Would that be possible? It was true that the master of Libya was all-powerful . . .

The woman drove her immediately to Bab al-Azizia, where a man, Saada Al Fallah, took her for a blood test right away, done by "a nurse from an Eastern country," who asked her to come back the next day. "It was odd, but I told myself that for a head of state one cannot be too careful." The following day, Brega, a uniformed bodyguard, took her directly to the Guide's bedroom. Several people were there pressing around him to show him photographs taken at the national holiday celebration. But they had barely left when he made insistent advances—which she refused—and then raped her without saying a word.

When she left the room in a state of shock, Saada Al Fallah showed no surprise at all and had no kind gesture for her. He handed her an envelope with one thousand dinars and said: "You're lucky to have been chosen. We intend for you to work for us." She wanted to have nothing to do with that and thought only of getting out of Bab al-Azizia. She even left Tripoli to go to her sister's in the south of Libya, worrying that someone might find her at her parents' house and relinquishing her hopes of going back to law school. But the family would soon be overwhelmed by other things. Khadija's brother, a student on Malta, was arrested for possession of narcotics when he returned to Libya. Drugs had apparently been slipped into his luggage and he might be getting the death sentence. The woman she had met at the hairdresser phoned Khadija and said: "You need to see Muammar. He is the only one who can save your brother's life."

Khadija realized this was blackmail. But she also knew that the regime wasn't concerned about any one life in particular. She returned to Tripoli and agreed to meet with Saada Al Fallah. "We can commute your brother's death sentence to fifteen years in prison—it's entirely within your power." In exchange Khadija would have to live at Bab al-Azizia, join the group of Gaddafi's (bogus) personal bodyguards, and give in to his wishes. Deathly afraid, she did, moving into the same basement where Soraya would later live, and joining a group of girls that, by her estimation, permanently numbered about thirty. Like Soraya, she was called at any hour of the day or night, watched the "deliveries" of young virgin girls who had no earthly idea of what they would have to endure, the brief visits of young men, and the endless little schemes of other women to acquire houses, cars, and money.

But very soon she would be given another mission: seducing a number of the regime's dignitaries, men who were reputed to be closest to the Guide, in order to trap them. They moved her into an apartment that she described as luxurious—"five-star quality"—within the compound of Bab al-Azizia, fully equipped with cameras. This is where she was to lure the individuals they pointed out to her, and sent in her direction, each time suggesting a ruse to use for coming on to them. It was her task to compromise them as seriously as possible by making them drink alcohol and sleep with her. The films would provide a means of blackmail, made available to the Guide. The names and information Khadija supplied, in great detail, were staggering and ran from the chief of the Libyan Information Department to this or that minister, colonel, general, or close cousin of Gaddafi's. The young woman affirmed she was also sent to Ghana and put up at the Golden Tulip Hotel with the mission to seduce the ambassador as well as the embassy's accountant.

As he usually did with most of his "daughters" (Khadija had the famous identity card), Gaddafi one day authoritatively assigned her a husband, chosen from among his guards. Khadija had no choice but to accept, though at least she would move back into the community of married women, which would make her more respectable in the eyes of Libyan society and of her family. She was hoping for a new life, wanted the illusion of a real marriage, and since she had a bit of money she went to a Tunisian clinic to have her hymen reconstructed. On the day of her wedding, as the guests hurried to her mother's house and her hands were being covered with henna, the telephone rang. It was Bab al-Azizia. The Guide demanded that she come to him immediately. She protested: "It is my wedding day!" They threatened her and so she went, but with a heavy heart. "He forced himself on me once again. He had to ruin that moment. He had to show he was still in control." Marriage changed nothing in their dynamic.

In February 2011, in the early days of the revolution, Saada Al Fallah paid her a visit with four soldiers and ordered her to make a declaration on a national television station stating that she was raped by a group of rebels. One might as well have dropped a bomb. Khadija belonged to the powerful tribe of the Warfalla. Publicly revealing a rape would be such an attack on the tribe's collective honor, would cause such a scandal that it would give rise to instant retaliations and would prevent the largest tribe of Libya from joining forces with the budding revolution.

But, above all, Khadija understood to what extent such a false confession would condemn her in everyone's eyes. "My own family would be responsible for killing me!" She refused. She was beaten, raped, burned with cigarettes. One of the guards broke her tibia with the steel heel of his boot, requiring one of Bab al-Azizia's doctors to come immediately. In the end she pretended to accept the order on the condition that they allow her to recuperate at her mother's house in the Tadjoura district. One night she managed to evade the surveillance of the guards who stood watch in front of the house and escaped in her nightgown via the back, with her passport. Rebels she met in her flight helped her to cross over into Tunisia, where she would stay throughout the revolution.

LEILA

Today Leila is about forty and feels like she is a survivor. She is married to a cousin who wedded her out of love, she is raising her children, and she lives with the dread that someday someone will discover the horrible secret that disrupted her youth. She wept while she told her story, a story she had never told before.

As an adolescent Leila had a schoolmate, the niece of a friend who was the right-hand man of Colonel Gaddafi, someone who had helped him take power during the coup d'état of September 1, 1969. Together they became active in one of the revolutionary committees and when her friend took the initiative one day to organize a meeting with the Guide for a school group, Leila was enthusiastic. A minivan brought the girls to Bab al-Azizia, where they were received in a large reception room on the second floor of what was then the Guide's residence and would be partially destroyed in the American bombing of 1986. Muammar Gaddafi was charismatic and attentive. Relaxed, he took his time to show interest in each one of the girls, asking them questions about their family background, their tribe, and their region. He laughed a lot and the girls were captivated by his charm.

Not long after this outing, a school employee came looking for Leila in her classroom and brought her to the office of the principal who, clearly very impressed, announced that a car from Bab al-Azizia was waiting in front of the school. Leila didn't understand why the car would be there but no one had any doubt that she should go with the driver. First she was taken to a room where she had to wait a moment and then Ahmed Ramadan, Gaddafi's personal secretary, brought her to the Guide's office. Dressed in a long white

Bedouin shirt, he came to meet her, complimented her on her beauty, and began to caress and grope her body. Bewildered, Leila froze, and when Gaddafi took her chest in his hands, she pulled back, screamed, shook him off, and ran. Ahmed Ramadan was waiting on the other side of the door. "Are you finished?" he asked in a neutral tone. Leila was in tears. "You must say goodbye to the Guide before you leave!" he insisted as he opened the door again to show the Colonel with an erection, laughing. The driver took her back to school. Principal and teachers asked no questions. She just noticed there were signs of a new respect.

That same evening Ahmed Ramadan phoned her at home. "It's a great honor that the Guide chose you. Your tears were ridiculous. The Guide simply wanted to be nice to you." Leila said nothing to her parents.

But a week later some members of one of the revolutionary committees ransacked the family home, supposedly looking for compromising documents. Leila's father, a member of the nobility, said to be a religious man, was humiliated, beaten, and dragged to the ground. The family was in shock.

Ahmed Ramadan called the next morning: "I heard what happened to your family. Rest assured: since you are working for the Guide, we will protect you." He told her he was sending a driver, whom she was to meet very close to her house. She felt trapped, invented a story to explain to her parents why she was going out, and found herself back at Bab al-Azizia in front of Gaddafi. "Did you see what happened to your family? It could turn out very badly. But it all depends on you: you can help them or you can cause them a lot of harm . . ."

"What do I have to do?"

"Well now! Be nice! I can tell that I really excite you."

He served her fruit juice, forced her to drink it, and kissed her greedily as he pressed himself against her, then disappeared.

The car came back for her a few days later. Ahmed Ramadan took her to a small reception room, where she waited, alone, for several hours. Then he took her to a library, where Gaddafi ended up, too. "I picked this setting for you, for I like students and books." Then he threw her down on a mattress and raped her. This was such a shock, such violence, that she thinks she lost consciousness. When she got her wits back, he was working at his desk and burst out laughing. "You'll like it later on!"

For three years he continued to have her brought to him and raped her. "I am the master of Libya. Every Libyan belongs to me, including you!" And: "You are my possession. And you should know that one of the verses of the Koran recognizes the master as having right over everything." It was three years of unremitting suffering, Leila recalls. She turned inward, missed school, let herself be punished and beaten at home for the absences she could no longer explain. Her parents thought she was living a depraved life, but the Guide kept repeating: "One single word about me and you'll never see your father again!" One day she told him she wasn't getting her period anymore, which didn't stop him from going at her one more time. But shortly thereafter Ahmed Ramadan handed her an envelope with some money and advised her to go to Malta. It was a minimal sum, nothing was arranged, and Leila herself had to find a hotel and a hospital. As he did the abortion, the doctor found her to be "in a sorry state" and suggested reconstructing her hymen a few days later. She was saved. Contrary to its usual modus operandi, Bab al-Azizia would never call for her again.

HOUDA

For several years Houda, too, was one of the countless involuntary mistresses of the Colonel who, without living at Bab al-Azizia, were called in at a moment's notice and whose lives were a living hell. In the nineties she was seventeen and preparing for her final exams with a group of classmates who often studied together, alternating homes. One day, a woman who was visiting the mother of one of the girls noticed her and bombarded her with compliments: "How beautiful you are!" Houda was extremely embarrassed and fled the woman's unrelenting gaze, but soon she ran into her once more and the woman began to praise her all over again: "I think you're marvelous. If you take that exam soon, I'll have a proposition for you." Very ill at ease, the girl assumed she was a matchmaker.

Not long thereafter Houda's brother was arrested. He never failed to attend the mosque so was suspicious in the eyes of the authorities. The scheming woman got in touch with the schoolgirl: "I know some people who can get your brother out of prison. Look here, I'll take you to them." She picked her up by car and brought her inside Bab al-Azizia. Clearly the woman was used to being there.

Houda was stunned. "Ah! Is this the new one?" a man in the front office exclaimed. Houda found the comment alarming but still had no clue. Ahmed Ramadan entered, saying: "Ah! Here's the girl whose brother is in such deep trouble! Now then, follow me!" He took them into a large office, where Muammar Gaddafi suddenly appeared. "Your brother is a traitor! I hope that you are a good revolutionary and won't turn out like him!" He came over to her, then ran his hands over her body before pressing himself against her. "However, I'll give your brother some thought, because I really find you magnificent." He kissed her neck, tried to reach for her breasts, and took out his penis. The girl fainted.

Crouching on the floor next to her, the woman tapped her on the face: "Wake up! You're being ridiculous! He is your master. This is your chance!" Gaddafi approached, wanted to touch her again, but she screamed and fought back. So he grabbed her by the clothes and hurled her brutally into a corner of the room. Wild, he seized the woman who'd brought Houda there and quickly penetrated her. He demolished the schoolgirl with a threatening look: "Next time it's you!"

In the car that took her home, Houda was too shocked to utter a word. But the woman explained to her: "The master has every right over us. He will make love to you, set your brother free, and you might get a scholarship for the university." The girl said nothing to her parents about what happened; it was impossible. But when her mother hit her, furious at her for being late, she simply told her some of the story, omitting any details: "I was arrested by the police and questioned about my brother."

Three days later, the woman phoned her: "I can't come with you to Bab al-Azizia but a car from protocol will come to pick you up. Think about your brother." So Houda found herself in front of Ahmed Ramadan, who interrogated her about the young man and took notes. It reassured her; perhaps her approach hadn't been in vain. But she was told she was to see the Guide again and was taken to his office, where he said: "You think a traitor is set free that easily? You're dreaming! It's not quite that simple. All the more so because you are a wild one! And will scream again if I touch you . . ."

"No, I don't want to upset you. But when can my brother leave prison?"

"You won't scream anymore? You promise?"

With a few rough movements he took off her clothes, threw her down on a mattress on the floor alongside a bookcase, and raped her. Then he left without a word.

Nobody came to see her or showed any concern for her. She didn't know how to get out and spent the rest of the night in his office, terrified. Ahmed Ramadan found her there the following day and took her to a room, where she had just begun to fall asleep when Gaddafi joined her, then raped her again, hitting and biting her. She was bleeding profusely and remained locked up there for two days, without food or drink. On the third day, Ahmed Ramadan sent her home, saying he'd be back in touch.

When she came home her parents were horrified by the state the girl was in and were sick with worry. She didn't want to talk but, since they hounded her with questions, she whispered that she had been at the police station. Alarmed, the family assumed that Houda's condition had to be connected to their son. They surrounded her, fussed over her, and insisted on taking her to the hospital.

There, a doctor examined her, and said: "You were raped."

"Yes, but I beg you, please don't say anything to my parents."

"You have to bring charges."

"No, impossible."

"Sexual relations outside of marriage is against the law, which forces me to report your case to the police."

"Do you really have a death wish?"

Gaddafi wouldn't leave Houda alone. For many long years, she had to submit to his demands, his madness, his brutalities, his fantasies. She could make no plans, living like a hermit, in perpetual fear that the scandal would be discovered. Her parents finally began to be suspicious, for the official cars were less and less discreet and Gaddafi demanded that she be present at his many speeches and lectures. That was when she discovered the horde of other women who were in the same position as she. They looked at each other but didn't talk. How to bring up the subject? Whom could they trust? One day he asked her to run up to him and kiss him in front of the cameras during a public event. He phoned her at night, threatened her, insisted she wear a specific outfit, kept her permanently available. She became depressed, suicidal, was disgusted with herself. But after several years, a suitor presented himself and she fell in love. Gaddafi was enraged, but she got married. And from then on she refused to go to Bab al-Azizia, despite the orders and her fear about what might happen to her. She was lucky. Many young husbands who hadn't been picked by the master would not survive their marriage to one of his favorites.

THE GENERAL'S WIFE
AND DAUGHTER

A general's daughter spoke out in the weekly newspaper *Libya Al Jadida*. Her testimony was confirmed by the editor in chief, Mahmoud Al Misrati. Colonel Gaddafi, who always inquired about the family situation of his subordinates and the appearances of their wives, found out one day that the wife of a general in his army was extremely beautiful. Did he give the orders himself? Or was it Mabrouka's idea? However it happened, three of his guards presented themselves one afternoon at the general's house to hand his wife an invitation to a women's reception organized by Safia Gaddafi for that very night.

The general was wary. He hadn't heard any mention of such an event and didn't at all like the thought of his wife going alone to Bab al-Azizia. Then one of the guards dialed a number and handed him his cell phone. Mabrouka was on the line. "It is a magnificent honor the Guide is doing you! It proves he knows you are close to him and considers you a true revolutionary. It will be a very fine party, strictly for wives." Reassured, the general let his wife go. When she returned a few hours later, she was strange and evasive. "Something in my mother seemed broken," her daughter says.

Other invitations followed, especially when the general was absent. After several months, the wife came home one day with the keys to a fine apartment. "A gift" from Safia Gaddafi, she said, announcing that they'd become great friends. The family moved, their lifestyle visibly improved; it was good to be in Gaddafi's good graces. But then one evening Mabrouka and two other women presented themselves at the door of the general's house, this time with an invitation for his daughter from Gaddafi's oldest daughter, Aisha. Her mother's face fell. Horrified, she held her hand over her mouth. Her daughter, on the other hand, was thrilled. "This evening? I'd be delighted! The only problem is that I have no evening gown."

"Don't worry, I came prepared!" Mabrouka said with a smile, then turned around and pointed to a suitcase. "Inside is everything you'll need to look beautiful tonight!"

The girl quickly put on the dress, applied makeup, and followed Mabrouka, not understanding why her mother had tears in her eyes when they parted. The general himself seemed taken aback. He would be even more shocked when, weeping, his wife admitted that Safia's invitations were cover-ups for her being summoned by the Guide and that the money, the gifts, the apartment were merely remunerations for a forced sexual relationship. The general blew up, bellowed, and decided to go immediately to Bab al-Azizia. But at that moment he collapsed and was taken to the hospital. He had suffered a stroke.

At the same time the general's daughter was surprised to see Gaddafi enter the room where she had been made to wait. "Where is Aisha?" she asked with a smile.

"I am Aisha," the Guide answered coldly. He didn't try to seduce her, or to be tactful, but instead raped, beat, and humiliated her as much and as often as he could. She didn't get out of Bab al-Azizia till a week later, when she went to the hospital to see her father, who was dying. His death would only make things easier for the Guide. When Mabrouka called to set up regular appearances for the daughter, she asked the mother to get her ready according to the Guide's taste—"You know what needs to be done"—and to cover her arms and legs with henna.

The stories are many and, in the West, it's hard to imagine what it costs these women to speak. Not only in terms of the trauma, which is the same everywhere, but in terms of the risks for them and their families. The chaos in which Libya finds

185

itself—it's filled with weapons—combined with the yoke of religion for the time being excludes any objective debate on the issue. It explains why, despite basic rules of journalism that require the identification of one's sources, I agreed to accept the requests of the majority of the women quoted in this book to preserve their anonymity.

3

THE AMAZONS

Colonel Gaddafi's female bodyguards—those whom the international press nicknamed "Amazons"—contributed a great deal to his legend and his media success. Undoubtedly, they left as much of an imprint on the minds of others as did his ever more eccentric attire, his rock star sunglasses, his tousled mop of hair, and his perpetually made-up, Botox-treated, cocaine-addicted face. They followed him everywhere, poured into the most varied uniforms, some of them armed, others not; their hair down to their shoulders or neatly tucked inside a beret, cap, or turban; often wearing makeup and earrings and pendants bearing the image of the Guide, their feet tucked in heavy-duty boots, high-heeled ankle boots, and, occasionally, pumps.

They served as his standard-bearers, a foil for him, attracting photographers and fascinating heads of state and ministers, who came to welcome him at the airport as he arrived or were received at Bab al-Azizia for an audience in the tent. Thus the former French minister of foreign affairs Roland Dumas was delighted to be escorted by some "very pretty armed young girls," and Silvio Berlusconi's lecherous smiles spoke volumes about his satisfaction on visits to Libya. But the message Gaddafi conveyed was extremely ambiguous.

Sure, it confirmed his singular eccentricity on the world stage. A megalomaniac and provocateur, the Colonel attached a great deal of importance to his image and to the staging of his appearances and speeches. On the one hand, he wanted to be known as unique, tolerated no competition or comparison, all but prohibited any name other than his own to emerge from his country (no Libyan writer, musician, athlete, merchant, economist, or politician could ever be recognized during his reign; soccer players could be identified only by the number on their jersey). So the idea of intriguing the entire world by presenting himself as the only head of state who had a completely female guard fulfilled this ambition.

It also seemed to put into practice his view of himself as the great liberator of women. How many conferences and rants must he have delivered on this theme? How many lessons must he have given to the West and the whole Arab world? A truth to be acknowledged by all: Colonel Gaddafi was "the friend of women." There was not a single trip into the regions of Libya, not a single tour abroad where this message was not hammered out at a meeting with some women's association.

He had already laid out a certain attitude toward women in the third volume of his famous *Green Book* (equality between the sexes, freedom from discrimination, the right to work for everyone on the condition that women's "femininity" be respected), but his intention was rapidly radicalized, leading in 1979 to the creation of a Military Academy for Women and, two years later, to a fiery and triumphant speech when the first to receive their degrees were presented before the country. This school, unique in the world, would be an enormous source of pride for Libya, he proclaimed. How daring the multitudes of young Libyan women who registered were, embodying the shining proof of how mentalities had changed. They had to continue!

Thus, on September 1, 1981, he made a great declaration: "The men and women of the Arab nations are subject to an attempt to subjugate their powers. But inside the Arab nation, women have actually been dominated by the forces of oppression, feudalism, and profit. We call for a revolution to liberate the women of the Arab nation, which will be a bomb to shake up the entire Arab region, inciting female prisoners, whether in palaces or marketplaces, to rebel against their jailers, their exploiters, and their oppressors. This call is certain to cause profound echoes and repercussions in the entire Arab nation and in the world at large. Today is not just any day, it is the beginning of the end of the era of harems and slaves and the beginning of women's liberation within the Arab nation." And so, women in arms appeared as the most beautiful jewel in the crown of the revolution. Entrusting them with his personal security was therefore more than symbolic. It was an act of faith in feminism. That, at least, is how Gaddafi's preference for female guards was frequently framed in the West. The irony is shocking.

Having an escort of Amazons flattered the Colonel's idea of himself as a seducer, feeding people's fantasies and suspicions. The cliché of the oriental harem was never far away—in sharp contrast to his feminist rhetoric—and was reinforced by the absence on the public stage of his legal wife, Safia Farkash, the official mother of seven of his children, whom he had married in 1971 (after a lightning-quick divorce from his previous wife). All these young women at his service, devoted to him, and ready to give up their lives for him . . . The message was, shall we say, blurred.

But who were they really, these girls in uniform, those close guards, those standard-bearers of the Guide? Soraya's account categorically denies the endless adulation these guards received, including the praise for their combat training and skill. Had she not been told to simply put on the uniform the very day after her kidnapping? Had she not, without consultation, been told she would join the "elite" corps, and instructed merely to mimic the other bodyguards on the Guide's trips, by looking busy and severe, like the guards on whom the master's life depended? "What a joke!" Soraya said, rolling her eyes. What a charade! My observation of a handful of Amazons, who accompanied the Colonel on a visit to Paris in December

2007, seemed to confirm these kinds of allegations. Perched on the roof of a sightseeing river boat, the guards took pictures of each other laughing like schoolgirls, and afterward went shopping on the Rue du Faubourg Saint-Honoré and the Champs-Elysées. No, these girls had not been trained at the Military Academy. Yes, they certainly were Gaddafi's mistresses and sexual objects. His favorites or his little slaves. Sayed Gaddaf Eddam, a cousin of the Guide's and a high-ranking military officer, told me from his prison in Misrata that he was "disgusted" by these women.

The investigation in Tripoli proved to be difficult. There was now no one who wanted to hear about the famous bodyguards. They had vanished with the Guide. Flown away! Any mention of them only prompted embarrassment and scorn—first of all, at the Libyan Ministry of Defense, at the entrance of which sits a carpet with the image of Gaddafi. "Their existence gravely damaged the image of the Libyan army," Oussama Jouili, commander of the rebels of the city of Zintan, who was named minister of defense after the Guide's death, assured me. "What a disgrace! And such a slap in the face for members of the real military, those who had a noble ideal of their profession and of the defense of their country! Gaddafi put them forward to attract the spotlight and refine his own image, but it was nothing but hypocrisy. At the same time he was destroying his own army. Unbearable! I was a young captain, and I reached the point of hating the whole institution of the army, and was ready to resign as soon as it was possible. Where were we heading? How could I take seriously those women who Gaddafi was simply throwing to the wolves? Who could imagine for even a second that he would trust them completely with his protection? Let's face it, they were there just for show, to play to the gallery, and—how shall I say it?—to brighten up his leisure time. It was revolting."

I saw the same reaction from Ramadan Ali Zarmouh, the president of the Military Council of Misrata, the third largest city in the country, and certainly one of the most ravaged by the war. He, too, had resigned from Gaddafi's army very early on, despite his rank as colonel. And, like the rebel commander Jouili, deplored the "masquerade" and the "pathetic theater" not only of the bodyguards but of all the female soldiers. "Poor girls! They landed among our ranks, fully inflated by the speeches of that bastard, who manipulated them to try to impress the world and satisfy his own desires! They were badly trained, badly prepared, and often didn't have their parents' blessing to be in the army. Besides, how could they have in good conscience accepted that their daughters would be thrown into this man's universe? In Libya this would be unthinkable. We saw them as victims behind whom [better trained] men inevitably had to be placed, while he was showing off, surrounded by mistresses and puppets untrained to defend him."

Radical judgments like these were shared by all the rebels and military men I was able to question. Was it machismo on their part? Yes, to some extent, since the integration of women in the army had never been truly accepted by the military hierarchy, nor by traditional Libyan society. It could be said that Gaddafi had probably gone too far too fast in a country where women were wives and mothers before all else and often confined to the house. From 1975 on, he had pushed the concept of "people at arms" and supported the idea that weapons should no longer be the monopoly of a classical army, destined to disappear, but ought to be put in the hands of all citizens— men and women—and that this should happen without delay. In 1978, he authorized a law that made military training for all compulsory in the secondary schools, for girls as well as boys. This caused a minor revolution since, to the utter amazement of their parents, the former had to wear combat fatigues and be taught by male teachers. "Combat fatigues worn by a woman is worth more than a silk outfit worn by an ignorant, inane, superficial bourgeois woman, unaware of the challenges that confront her and, consequently, her children," the Guide once declared. When in 1979 he created the Military Academy for Women, he sent hordes of especially aggressive recruiters to girls' schools. It had to be done fast. Liberated women in arms would be Gaddafi's best propaganda. Three months of training for female soldiers, recruited after the third year of secondary school; two years for female officers, selected after the baccalaureate diploma. Finally, in 1981, he launched the idea of a movement of so-called revolutionary nuns, open to all women, both civil and military, who would be "the elite of the elite."

In order to be accepted into this group, the women had to renounce marriage and devote their entire lives exclusively to the defense of the revolution—in other words, devote themselves to the Guide. That was his greatest fantasy. In a speech he gave on February 13, 1981, to the pioneers of the revolutionary women's movement, in referring to Christian nuns "who dress in white, the symbol of purity, and who devote themselves entirely to the ideal of Christ," Muammar Gaddafi was deliberately provocative. "Why do Christian women become nuns while you sit still and remain spectators? Can Christian nuns be greater than the Arab nation?" He concluded: "It is through renunciation that the revolutionary nun is holy, pure, and places herself above ordinary individuals so she can be closer to the angels."

I met no revolutionary nuns. Even in Gaddafi's time they had already disappeared into the society at large, and nobody has managed to estimate their number. There's no point in stating that no one today claims that title. But I did interview two women colonels who had each responded to the Guide's call at a very young age and wholeheartedly joined the army. Quickly disappointed, one of them affirmed having wished for Gaddafi's deposition and after his death discovered a certain renewal of interest in her profession. Now in prison waiting to go to court for murders committed during the civil war, the other one fluctuates between nostalgia and anger.

It took many days to convince Colonel Fatima to talk. On the face of it, she had no reason to blame herself for anything.

But here she was: a soldier who had believed in the Guide's message and became one of the dupes of history. Despite the propaganda, the Libyans had never felt any sympathy for the female soldiers; since the revolution of 2011 they were overtly expressing their feeling of repulsion. So it wasn't easy for the unfortunate survivors of the Gaddafi era; they had no desire whatsoever to put themselves forward. And yet Fatima refused the idea that women should be forever banned from the army and that the Guide's atrocities and duplicity should provide the opportunity for them to be disqualified. It was both unjust and insulting.

An imposing woman in her fifties, wrapped in a large red coat with a black veil around her plump face, her bearing a little tense, Fatima finally came to my hotel room in Tripoli one evening. The place was inconspicuous and neutral. After years of propaganda, she said, the time had surely come to speak the truth.

"The recruiters who came to my high school in the late seventies enthralled me: the idea they presented about military engagement was so dazzling that I could only see my future as in the army. Nothing could be more exalting than defending one's country, and having men and women united and equal. What an awe-inspiring idea, and how revolutionary! All the more so because these recruiters cited the example of the Algerian revolution in which young women like Djamila Bouhired had taken all sorts of risks as liaison officers, planting bombs and fighting battles in order to liberate their people. They were magnificent people, heroines. Women were raising their heads. I was dreaming of a similar involvement." Military training had just started to get considerable emphasis at the school. Physical exercises, handling of weapons, lectures, exams . . . Fatima committed herself wholly to it, convinced she would thereby be part of the "armed people" of whom Gaddafi used to speak. Her parents, on the other hand, were scandalized that high school girls could be asked to dress in male uniforms; it was so improper. "Libyan society wasn't ready for it," she said. "But we, the young, we took the bait. And then, once military service became obligatory again, and every Libyan had to devote several weeks a year to being trained, we were all forced to take part in the project. Every Libyan had their reservist's card." In reality, traffic in these cards allowed the wealthiest people to avoid these exercises, but at the time she didn't know that.

So in 1980 Fatima entered the Military Academy of Tripoli, which was then only in its second year. There she met girls from Egypt, Lebanon, Algeria, and Sudan. The teachers were basically still all men and the courses were demanding: Morse code, cartography, secretarial work, military tactics, weapons handling, maneuvers training, including during the night and in stormy weather. "But it was worth it! We were a world attraction. Television crews came from all over. We felt like we were growing wings. We were the future. We were modern!" Obviously, with every speech Gaddafi gave the women became more galvanized. He was their champion and they didn't doubt his readiness to change the lives of all Libyan women and, one day, to push a few of them to the rank of general.

Then there was the graduation ceremony and the marching parade, repeated a thousand times. "I was too exhausted to listen to the Guide's speech all the way to the end." But it took no more than a month for Fatima to grow disenchanted. "We had been had. The promises were nothing but lies. Gaddafi spurned his own army and obviously expected nothing from women—they were just images by which to create his myth . . . and a breeding ground for mistresses." Fatima was named an officer in a school near Bab al-Azizia, where she was officially in charge of the daily military training, but "the daughters of the Gaddafi clique" performed arrogantly. "I wore a uniform but had a title stripped of any power." She was then transferred to army headquarters. In the morning a driver would pick her up, but she had no role to play and remained underpaid. "So gradually the girls in my year grew bitter. Our study was nothing but a fraud; the love for the nation died. We told ourselves that our lives were a failure! I stopped wearing the uniform, forgot my service number, was no longer in shape, and disregarded everything I'd learned in school. I wouldn't even have been able to take a Kalashnikov apart anymore."

Obviously, if she had been incorporated as one of the bodyguards she would have had a few advantages, especially those of travel and money. But you had to be tall and beautiful, have long hair, and be deemed eye-catching by Gaddafi's first circle or by the Guide himself. This is what had happened to Salma of Soraya's story, who was noticed during a visit to her city of Zliten. "Gaddafi's bodyguards were not a true corps. It was just a collection of girls from Special Forces, the revolutionary guards, the police academy, the Military Academy, the revolutionary nuns, and his mistresses of the moment. Gaddafi used them as he pleased and no one had any chance of resisting, even less of complaining. The most cunning ones managed to take advantage of it and were given cars and houses. But, please, forget the image of an elite corps! It was just any old group, a mere show in which Gaddafi made sure he included a few black women to demonstrate he wasn't racist and keep some doors in Africa open. The real guards on whom his personal security rested didn't appear in this picture. They were men from Sirte, his native city."

Early in 2011 Fatima was excited to see the insurrection against Gaddafi make headway. She officially joined the revolutionary movement on March 20, making her Kalashnikov "available to the rebels." But she stayed within the system, gathering as much information as she could and distributing tracts in the army offices. "Desertion was not an option, or else my parents and I would be in a communal grave today." When I spoke with her, she was part of the military corps led by Abdelhakim Belhadj, the commander of the Military Council of Tripoli, and said she had gotten some of her drive back and had renewed faith in her profession. But she knew it would take time to repair the damage and restore credit to the women in uniform.

I met another female colonel in the prison of Zawiya, a small town on the coast about fifty kilometers from Tripoli. At first she refused to give me her name, but at the end of the interview she unexpectedly told it to me, gave it to me like a pledge of trust. A gift. "Fine then! My name is Aicha Abdousalam Milad. Goodbye!" The cell, in the back of a small courtyard, was painted yellow and had an iron door with a huge deadbolt lock, an obstructed window, and two places to sleep: a mattress right on the floor and a metal bed that had seen better days. A dim lightbulb dangled from a wire running along a side wall, a small electric radiator stood in a corner, and a kettle soon provided some hot water for tea. I was surprised at first to see two people in this minuscule room, and assumed that both were prisoners, but the woman who seemed most miserable, huddled up on the bed, her eyes deep in their sockets and her expression one of exhaustion, explained that she was the guard. Having slept in her car for five years—"Nobody wanted to rent a room to a poor woman by herself!"—she now preferred to share the cell with her prisoner.

In contrast, Aicha looked in very good shape. Tall and slender, her hair held together in a turban, she had a refined face, a beauty spot on her left cheek, and was wearing a striped sweatshirt under a black velvet outfit with athletic elegance. Sitting cross-legged on her mattress, she agreed to talk about the path she'd taken but insisted on having things be clear from the start: she was a professional army woman—"This is my calling in life!"—but had never belonged to the Gaddafi "clique," nor to his bodyguards. Once this point was settled, she could disclose the passion she'd felt for the army at a very young age, the fateful encounter with the recruiters visiting her school in Sebha, a town in the Saharan desert and a stronghold of the Gaddafi tribe, and how she had joined the Military Academy for Women at the end of December 1983. Like most of the students, she came from a large family (nine children) of modest income, with parents who had been extremely reluctant to have a daughter in uniform. "We all had to force the issue. But what bliss! Half of the army had to be composed of women or the concept would make no sense. Gaddafi finally had shown confidence in girls and brought them out of the house!"

At the same time, Aicha managed to get her nursing degree, and when she graduated from the Academy in 1985 she was assigned to her native south to train other girls and was rapidly promoted. Returning to Tripoli twenty years later, she joined the management of the revolutionary guards, whose duty it was to protect the Guide, and found herself in charge of the regular selection of his bodyguards. "What a responsibility! They were the ones who were going to show the whole world that Libyan women were armed and respected. They played the role of ambassadors! I couldn't make any mistakes!" So, she said, she chose the "spectacular" ones. Meaning what? The girls who were "endowed with charisma." Prettiness "wasn't the point. I wanted them to have a presence, be impressive. And I preferred them tall, otherwise I made them wear high heels." Every girl dreamed of being chosen and begged Aicha to let them be in the limelight one day. "It could turn their life upside down, especially if they weren't professional soldiers. They accompanied the Guide when he traveled, received envelopes with a lot of money. So—please believe it—once they were in place, they pulled out all the stops to measure up. Beautiful makeup, impeccable dress . . . They knew very well that all the cameras were fixed on them."

Aicha didn't want to talk about Gaddafi's behavior with his bodyguards. That was top secret. She did her job, suggesting girls. What happened to them afterward was no concern of hers. She also refused to discuss Mabrouka, the only one behind the Guide who didn't wear the uniform but whose importance in the organization of the female entourage was no secret. "I don't want to be likened to that. My pitiful salary —832 dinars a month [about 500 euros]—proves I had nothing to do with the clique and the business of the bodyguards!" With an odd gesture, she suddenly pulled a little ring from her ear and handed it to me: "You see this? It isn't even gold! Many of the bodyguards made a fortune. I, I have nothing!" Not even freedom.

What she was left with was honor, she said. The pride of having held high the banner of the Libyan woman warrior. She proclaimed her unbroken loyalty to her leader and his army during the last war. She had conscientiously obeyed orders and fought the insurrection—behaved like "a professional," without a trace of regret. The head of the prison, a rebel who subsequently insisted on having me visit the sinister mausoleum of Zawiya dedicated to the martyrs of the revolution, had a very different view. He accused her of having tortured and killed prisoners herself. Although the majority of the female soldiers would be released, Aicha, who was captured on August 21, would be waiting a long time before her case came to court.

"The situation of the military women under Gaddafi was sad and pathetic," Najwa al-Azrak, the vice minister of social affairs in charge of the dossier, would later tell me. "For the Guide the Military Academy was a ruse by which he gained access to women. And then, as he gradually found other ways to get them, he lost interest and the school deteriorated." Nevertheless, during the civil war, in desperation the regime mobilized countless women soldiers who until then had been neglected and kept in barracks. Some were sent into combat with mercenaries, among whom there were women as well. During the siege of Tripoli, others were sent to the many checkpoints in the city to verify identities and search vehicles, or were put in the humiliating situation of having to direct the long waiting lines for gas, a whistle between their lips. Puppets of Gaddafi, symbols of his regime, they were hated by the rebels and by the Libyan population at large. Some of them deserted and, when caught or betrayed, paid with their lives or by being raped for their support of the revolution. There were also those who were taken as a group to places near the front to "satisfy the desire" of male battalions.

The fate of most of Gaddafi's bodyguards threatens to remain unknown. Bodies found in the rubble of Bab al-Azizia seem to indicate that several of them were liquidated in August, in the regime's very last hours. At the moment of the debacle and the Guide's desperate flight, they were of no further use.

4

THE PREDATOR

Never could Dr. Faisal Krekshi have imagined what he was to discover when he and a handful of rebels took control of the University of Tripoli in late August 2011. Not that this calm, levelheaded, fifty-year-old professor and gynecologist, who had been trained in Italy and then at the Royal College of London, was ignorant of the corruption in the university system, of the networks of surveillance and denunciation put in place by the revolutionary committees, of the immense instrument of propaganda wielded by the various departments. He knew how fresh the memory of the public hangings of students in 1977 and 1984 still was among the Libyan people, and he was aware that no university career could be envisioned without pledging complete loyalty to the regime.

So, after a night of intense fighting on the campus, he wasn't surprised to find an improvised prison inside some shipping containers, an office for the dreaded head of the security services, Abdallah Senoussi, as well as drawers jampacked with information on dozens of students and professors, including a list of individuals to be executed. But what he found by accident, as he was searching the nooks and crannies of the university looking for possible snipers and forcing the doors of a secret apartment in the "green auditorium" where Muammar Gaddafi liked to give speeches, went far beyond his worst suspicions.

A vestibule adjoined a huge reception room furnished with brown leather armchairs. Then a hallway led up to a windowless wood-paneled bedroom. A double bed had been made, covered with a quilted blanket, surrounded by cheap floral patterned rugs and two small bedside tables with lamps that spread an orange light. Next to the bedroom was a bathroom with a shower, a toilet, a bidet, and a Jacuzzi with a gilded faucet. It was strange to find what looked like a bachelor pad in a building reserved for study and for the teaching of the *Green Book*. But the next room completely baffled visitors and chilled me to the bones when I had the chance to explore the place myself. Across from the bedroom a door opened out onto a perfectly equipped gynecological examination room, including a bed with stirrups, a projector, X-ray equipment, medical instruments, and laminated directions in English.

Although otherwise completely restrained, Dr. Krekshi couldn't hide his disgust. "How could one not be shocked and overcome," asked the well-known specialist who had been named as rector of the university after the revolution. "Nothing, absolutely nothing, could possibly justify the presence of such a setup. If any emergency was ever to be expected, the center of obstetrics and gynecology was less than a hundred meters away. So why this? What illegal and perverse practices had been hidden from view here? There are two possibilities I can think of: interrupting pregnancies and reconstructing hymens, both of which are forbidden in Libya. And without uttering the word 'rape,' I feel compelled to think of some very disturbing sexual behavior."

He spoke in a serious voice, weighing every word, mindful of the horror of his discovery. He told me that he had been the official gynecologist of Gaddafi's daughters Aisha and Hana. "It puts me in a strange position," he acknowledged with an apologetic smile. "The Gaddafi family respected my expertise, and I asked for nothing more. Occasionally, the daughters would express their father's amazement at me. 'He's not demanding a car? A house?' No, I wanted nothing. Nothing!" He was familiar with Muammar Gaddafi's appetite for young girls. He had heard about what he called "the magic touch," that hand he would place on the head of his prey as a signal to his bodyguards. And he, who taught family planning and each year devoted an entire course to the notion of "taboo," was well aware that Gaddafi's sexual mores fell under the greatest of all taboos. No one would have risked mentioning the subject, alerting the female students, or organizing a security cordon. They preferred not to know anything.

As for Gaddafi's victims, they could only keep silent and inconspicuously leave the university. This meant it was impossible to estimate the numbers of those invited to Bab al-Azizia and those taken to the presidential suite concealed beneath the amphitheater. The day of his ghastly discovery, Dr. Krekshi told me he'd found "eight or nine" DVDs in the apartment with videos of sexual attacks perpetrated by the Guide. But he admitted he had destroyed them immediately. I was dumbfounded. Destroyed? Were they not crucial forms of evidence? "Think of the circumstances. The war was still on. I couldn't guarantee that these videos would never fall into irresponsible or dangerous hands, that they wouldn't facilitate coercion or blackmail. My first concern was to protect the girls." A strange reaction. It was a heavy responsibility, but shouldn't it be up to a court of justice to make such a decision?

The revelation that Gaddafi had a secret apartment right in the middle of the university created shock waves on campus. But this didn't mean that people's tongues were loosened. They reviled the dictator and, proclaiming their loathing, gleefully trampled on his posters, which were now used as doormats in front of the classrooms. Yet the veiled female students kept walking and ignored me when I tried to find out more, and one young man I'd asked to conduct a poll on the subject sent me a text message: "I'm calling it off. It's taboo." Really! There had to be witnesses, people who'd noticed suspicious goings-on or had heard talk of young girls being harassed! Was there really nobody who was willing to criticize the system?

The young editor in chief of the weekly *Libya Al Jadida* seemed to be the only one willing to break the silence. "I had a friend, a girl from a farmer's family in the region of Azizia, who came to study medicine in Tripoli," he told me. "During one of his visits to the university Gaddafi put his hand on her head and his bodyguards arrived at her house the next day to tell her that the Guide had chosen her to be a revolutionary guard. The family refused, so her brother was threatened, and after that she agreed to meet with the Guide, was raped and held captive for a week, then was let go with a packet of money. Her parents were too humiliated to take her back. Returning to the university was inconceivable for her. She was lost. Today she officially works in the automobile business, but I know for a fact that she lives by selling her body."

With her light complexion, long curly hair down to her shoulders, and haughty demeanor, Nisreen isn't surprised. Raised in Libya in a middle-class family, with one European parent, she knew it would be impossible for her to survive in the oppressive, hypocritical atmosphere of the Gaddafi regime and that she would be better off studying abroad. "Nothing could be further from our minds than the possibility of rape," she told me one evening, "even though the escapades of the Guide's sons and their gang were known by everyone. But sooner or later every girl was confronted with sexual exploitation. Women sent by Bab al-Azizia would crisscross the campus, install themselves in restrooms where girls were quietly doing their makeup, join their conversations, and quite quickly make propositions, including those of a financial nature."

And it wasn't only the dark shadow of Bab al-Azizia. The whole university was drenched in an atmosphere of sexual blackmail. "You can't count the girls who failed their exams because they refused their professor's advances. Or those who were aghast at their grades and then found they were being offered some very private courses. I heard of girls who gave themselves to the professor of their fiancé so that he would get his diploma, an indispensable precondition of their marriage. I've seen boys ask their girlfriend to do this and then, sometimes, break up with her afterward. Sex was a means of exchange, a means of promotion, and an instrument of power. The Guide's mores turned out to be contagious. His mafia operated in the same way. The system was corrupt down to the bone."

Alarmed by the organization he uncovered as he took over the university's reins, Dr. Krekshi confirmed that this went on. It was an utterly broken system, with networks and spies in each department and administrative office, and coordinated by the institution's secretariat in collaboration with Bab al-Azizia. The objective? To select the prettiest female students, under any pretext, and lead them first into the Guide's net, then into that of his clique. Good grades, diplomas, prestigious assignments, study grants—everything was in their grasp as long as they remained meek and docile. The gifts could, of course, go beyond the scholarly and might include things like iPhones, iPads, cars, and jewelry. The bids could run very high for the most desirable girls who, generally speaking, didn't come from poor backgrounds.

"It's the law of silence: no one will ever testify to rape," the doctor told me. However, he did allude to several stories that are illustrative of the practices in place—for instance, that of a female student registered at the medical school who found herself in the paramedical curriculum. "Given her excellent grades, it was incomprehensible. She asked for an explanation from the university secretary, who promised her the error would be corrected on the condition that she go to Regatta, the leisure center on the coast where the regime's dignitaries, and especially their sons, gave themselves over to all sorts of vice. The whole of Tripoli knew about Regatta. It was an area without any laws, where everything was legal. The girl refused and for two years kept getting zeros on every exam. Can you imagine the pressure? Finally, I myself wrote a letter to get her transferred back into the medical school. In my new role I've passed on five more testimonies by brave young women that prove the abject corruption of the system."

The apartment hidden on the ground floor of the *Green Book* Academy will keep its secrets forever. Apparently, there are other niches the Guide frequented that were set up especially for him, because he always needed sex partners, male and female, preferably young virgins. Khadija, the student who was raped and stayed at Bab al-Azizia for several years, forced to trap different men in the regime, assured me that Gaddafi wanted at least four a day. That number was confirmed in the British press by Faisal, an attractive young man also spotted by the Guide at the university. He was forced to interrupt his law studies in order to enter Gaddafi's private service immediately. "The girls would go into his bedroom, he'd do his business, and he'd come out as if he'd merely wiped his nose." Thirty years old today, the young man emphasized Gaddafi's violence and his enormous consumption of Viagra, and confirmed that countless women "would go straight from his room to the hospital," victims of internal injuries. That is Soraya's testimony, and is confirmed by several others I spoke with. Not only was Gaddafi insatiable but he was sadistic and extremely brutal as well.

So, for him, schools and universities were perpetually restocked, natural fishponds. It was at the University of Benghazi that the Colonel also spotted Houda Ben Amer, the mother of his adopted daughter Hana. She was originally from Benghazi and had gained national notoriety when, during a public hanging of a young pacifist opponent, she came out of the crowd of spectators, all worked up and excited, and pulled at the legs of the young man with all her might to hasten his death. That cruelty gave her the nickname "Houda the executioner," for the scene had been aired on national television. But

Gaddafi had noticed her long before that. In 1976, proclaiming her attachment to the regime, she opposed the April student demonstrations and supported the repression, denouncing and hunting down any opponents and leading "purification" campaigns at the head of revolutionary committees. A fellow student remembers, "We'd never seen a girl so aggressive, so ambitious, and with such nerve. She would take the floor to make scathing speeches, participate in meetings until deep into the night, and relay Gaddafi's messages while threatening any dissidents with more executions."

After the hangings of 1977, with the support of the Colonel, and speaking on his behalf, she continued to increase her power. Early on, she all but took control of the university, ousting professors and students she considered too far removed from the regime's orthodoxy. Then she vanished from Benghazi for a while, going to live with the Guide and joining his personal guard, and returned more influential than ever before, intimately linked to Gaddafi, who decided to marry her off (he himself was her witness) and appointed her to important functions: mayor of Benghazi, president of the Arab Parliament, president of the National Audit Office, minister. She became one of Libya's wealthiest women and was widely hated by the Libyan people. Her house in Benghazi was burned by the rebels during the first few hours of the insurrection, and she is today in prison in Tripoli, where she admitted to her jailers that she had been forced to abandon her little daughter—the result of her liaison with Gaddafi. The girl was born on November 11, 1985, if I can believe the photocopy of a 2007 passport I obtained, and was later adopted from an orphanage in Tripoli by Gaddafi's wife, Safia.

Every place where women regularly spent time was a potential source of women for the Guide, including prisons, where one of his bodyguards was at one point seen taking photographs of attractive detainees. Hairdressing salons and beauty parlors were a favorite locale and were diligently visited by Gaddafi's scouts. Wedding celebrations were another. He loved going to festivities where women were dressed in their most beautiful finery. If he couldn't get there himself, he would send his representatives and spend an insane amount of time looking over the photos and videos they'd take. A photographer from central Tripoli confirmed this, saying that he would always find a thousand pretexts not to submit any of the copies of wedding photos and videos he was asked for to Bab al-Azizia. Young girls confirmed that they had avoided certain parties at large hotels in Tripoli, afraid to be filmed and singled out for the Guide or his clique later on. Some parents lived in the same fear, forbidding their daughters—already deprived of social encounters—to go to parties or parades, especially if they were taking place anywhere near Bab al-Azizia. The Guide's residence, although protected like a fortress, would endlessly receive school groups and young activists. It was a godsend for Gaddafi.

His employees—drivers, guards, soldiers—were often called on to bring him photos and videos of their weddings. At first, some of them were quite touched by the Guide's interest, but they all became disillusioned. If a guest, a sister, a cousin had the misfortune of pleasing Gaddafi, the employee was instructed to arrange for a meeting. But if it was the young bride who caught the master's eye, the employee would find out only after the fact, when it was too late. The Colonel would manage to get him away from his home under the pretext of some mission, and then take advantage of his absence to summon the wife or pay her a visit, one that would lead to rape if the woman resisted. I cannot say how many terrible stories I was told about guards who, after their young wives confessed to them, were made crazy with rage, spite, jealousy and then, known to be seeking revenge against the Guide, were murdered on his orders. Several were hanged, others were cut up in pieces. Two of them had their limbs tied to cars that would drive in opposite directions. The scene was filmed and shown to newly hired guards so they would understand what price they'd pay if they betrayed the master of Bab al-Azizia.

Nurses, teachers, pediatric nurses were equally targeted. The director of a Tripoli day care center told me how one of her pretty employees was visited one day by three Amazons who asked her to join a team of young women selected to go to the airport with flowers to welcome a delegation from South Africa. "Make sure you look beautiful!" A few days later they came by to pick her up in a minibus that suddenly veered off the airport road and headed toward Bab al-Azizia instead. The group was surprised and thrilled when the Guide received them right away and improvised a little speech. But when everyone went back to the bus, the baby nurse found herself taken to a small room with a Jacuzzi, where two nurses rapidly did a blood test on her. Then, no longer smiling, Gaddafi reappeared. His intentions were very clear. The girl panicked: "I beg you, don't touch me. I come from the mountains. And I have a fiancé!" The Guide answered: "I'll give you a choice. Either I kill him or I let you marry him and give you a house, and you'll belong to both of us."

One of the dictator's close collaborators, a man who worked alongside him every day but had no decision-making powers, finally agreed—with enormous reluctance—to broach the subject with me. At first he denied knowing anything at all about what he called "the brother-Guide's private life" and refused to get mixed up in it: "I didn't stay around at night and I swear I never set foot in the basement of his residence." It was a nice way of stating that this place was where all danger lurked. But when I promised him that I wouldn't mention his name, he gradually began to trust me and in the end mentioned the service of "procurers" responsible for "answering the sexual needs" of the dictator. "They were pitiful and spineless sycophants, who groveled before him and fought to anticipate his desires." And then he summarized the situation. "Muammar Gaddafi," he said, could be described as a sexual obsessive—"It is all he seriously thought about"—and this "pathological" addiction led him to analyze everything via the prism of sex. "He governed, humiliated, subjugated, and sanctioned through sex."

But he had two different kinds of prey. The run-of-the-mill women who made up his daily diet were usually young, had simple backgrounds, and were found by what was known as his "special service," which was close to the Department of Protocol, and which during its final years was directed by the horrible Mabrouka Sherif, the Mabrouka so often mentioned in Soraya's account. He'd take these girls, most often by force—a few of them, those who had been particularly well indoctrinated, said they were flattered to have been "opened" by the Guide—and would generously reward those who satisfied him or who agreed to come back and recruit new girls. And then there were the others. The ones he aspired to have. The ones whose conquest and domination would be a personal challenge for him. Those who would be trophies of the most extraordinary type.

He showed great patience and strategy in wooing those women, and also expended enormous resources. There were the stars, of course—singers, dancers, actresses, and television journalists from the Near and Middle East. He sent planes across the globe to pick them up and cover them with riches and jewels even before they arrived. They satisfied his narcissism—the idea that he could have anyone he wanted—but that was not what interested him most. What really excited him was the idea of possessing the daughters or wives of powerful figures or of his opponents, whether it be for an hour, a night, or a few weeks. It was not so much about seducing a woman as, through her, humiliating the man who was supposed to be responsible for her—there is no greater shame in Libya—trampling him, annihilating him, or, if the secret never came out, having ascendancy over him, consuming his power and dominating him, at least psychologically.

"That Bedouin son, born in a tent, had suffered poverty and disregard throughout his childhood, and was motivated only by the thirst for revenge," was how his former collaborator put it to me. "He despised the rich and did his best to impoverish them. He hated aristocrats and the upper class—those individuals who naturally had what he would never have: culture, power, and good manners—and he vowed to humiliate them. By necessity that would happen via sex." He was able to coerce certain ministers, diplomats, and high-ranking military men to have sexual relations with him. "They had no choice—refusing would mean the death sentence—and the act was so shameful that not one of them would either complain or boast about it." Sometimes he commanded them to deliver their wives to him. If not, he'd make sure to trap the women—invite them to Bab al-Azizia when their husbands were away, or visit them himself, provoking their confusion and panic.

"But he really outdid himself in his schemes to get their daughters," the man went on. "It could be a long-term project, taking time to collect information and photographs of them—finding out about their tastes, their habits, their daily outings; approaching them, then encircling and getting close to them, with the help of his famous guards and their madam mother. They'd tell these daughters how much the Guide admired them. They'd flash money, a car—a BMW or a large 4x4—before their eyes, a medical degree if they were studying, or an office in town if they were dreaming of getting established. Everything was possible." What a victory when they finally came to him! What a hold over the man who had sired them!

5

MASTER OF
THE UNIVERSE

Among the dictator's luxurious delicacies, the "prey" he most coveted were the wives and daughters of monarchs and heads of state. For want of becoming "King of kings of Africa," as he desired, Gaddafi could at least dream of possessing their wives, one way of superseding them all. But in that realm it was unthinkable to resort to coercion and force. It required savoir faire, diplomacy, and tact. And spending lots and lots of money. Many wives understood very quickly that they could get anything from the Guide and didn't hesitate to ask for a meeting so that they could seek a donation from him for a hospital, a foundation, or some other project that was dear to their heart. He distributed money to all and sundry and, of course, managed to have it work to his own advantage.

Some daughters of African heads of state, whose morals were more liberated than those of Libyan women and who were used to living it up, made sure he would invite them to Tripoli, not hesitating to ask "Papa Muammar" to finance their vacation, study, or business enterprise. The Guide's office and then his bedroom were open to them. The daughter of a former president of Niger was one of these women, and she entered his private life for quite a long time, accompanying him on many official visits. But the Colonel also liked to take risks and seduce wives right under their husbands' noses. The great international summits offered him the opportunity to display all his talents.

One woman in her forties, who worked in the Department of Protocol for several years, made an appointment with me in a tea salon in an elegant section of Tripoli. A friend had told her about my investigation and she agreed to participate, something totally unexpected after all the refusals I had systematically received. Short and slender, very vivacious, she wore no veil and looked me straight in the eye, both friendly and assertive. "I feel it is my duty to speak with you," she said. "I wasn't able to take part in the revolution or take up arms against Gaddafi. I swear to you that I would have liked to do so. Meeting with you, contributing anything that will help the truth come out about what the regime really was, that's one way of adding my bit to the revolution."

She admitted how disillusioned she'd been since she'd enlisted in the Department of Protocol. How she, too, had lost any illusions about the Guide and the mechanisms that made him tick. She had thought she was working for Libya, serving a grand design led by a visionary with integrity. Instead, she found herself running headlong into a system of payoffs, sycophants, and sexual corruption that obliterated all her convictions.

She had tried to hold her own, to be irreproachable in her own work. But it didn't take her long to discover that Gaddafi's obsession with sex impaired the managing of the whole regime and could shatter the entire meticulous organization of summits and visits by state leaders of which her department was in charge. She was appalled. "He was playing with fire. We were constantly brushing up against a diplomatic incident. Every rule was disregarded. The wife of one head of state was said to have a strong interest in schools. It was our task to arrange a schedule for her that would meet her expectations, including meetings with educational professionals and visits to various institutions. Yet on D-day the carefully planned schedule exploded: a car from Bab al-Azizia came to pick up the lady in question for a 'private interview' with the Guide. An interview! Of course, that made no sense whatsoever. But I soon understood. Better to forget the school. The next day, the woman received a suitcase containing five hundred thousand dollars in banknotes and a gold or diamond necklace, I forget which."

In November 2010, the third summit of the African-European Union was organized in Tripoli. The Department of

Protocol thus had the responsibility of arranging the welcome of the wives of the heads of state, as well as organizing the various activities that might please them. A small file was prepared on each one of them, containing her photograph and a CV. A female companion was assigned to them as they toured around. The day of their arrival Mabrouka Sherif appeared in the office of the airport director, where the files were stored. She scrutinized the photograph of each First Lady, and stopped at one of them, a particularly magnificent woman who sported an awe-inspiring mane of hair. "Make me a photocopy of her record. It's for the Guide."

The first day all went as planned, with each delegation going to its respective lodgings at night. The following day, Mabrouka called the Department of Protocol: "Come with me to deliver the gifts." Accordingly, a car made a tour of the hotels and luxurious residences where the different delegations were staying. And a protocol employee discovered the expensive nature of the presents with the same astonishment as did some of the wives. "I really thought I'd seen it all, but this . . . I couldn't get over it! Incredible, dazzling necklaces, and other things besides! When you see what we bought for the woman in the photograph . . ." Indeed, when Mabrouka presented her jewelry box to this particular lady, a wife of an African head of state famous for her love of luxury and her flamboyant flirtatiousness, everyone's eyes opened wide: the diamond necklace was enough to take your breath away. "I didn't think anything like that existed. It was like a necklace out of science fiction."

Mabrouka whispered: "The Guide would like to see you." And the lady complied.

That evening there was a grand dinner at the Rixos Hotel, the five-star palace of Tripoli. Gaddafi was holding court in the center of a U-shaped arrangement of tables, surrounded by the heads of state. The women were seated at three round tables. As if by accident, Mabrouka had taken a seat near the splendid wife. At the end of the dinner, as everyone was getting up from the table, she took the woman by the hand and worked it so they would cross the path of the Guide, who stopped her, of course, and greeted her with a thousand compliments. At two in the morning, Mabrouka called the protocol employee: "What time does this woman's plane leave?"

"At ten in the morning."

"I will send you a car. Make sure she is at Bab al-Azizia at nine."

"Out of the question. Tomorrow morning I have to oversee the departures of all the delegations, and I'll really be too busy with other things."

"Fine, I'll take care of it myself. But be sure her plane is delayed."

At ten that morning the husband was waiting for his wife in one of the airport halls. At eleven she still hadn't arrived. Nor at noon. The employees of protocol and of the delegation were obviously highly embarrassed. Unconcerned and smiling, the wife arrived at one-thirty, the zipper on the side of her sheath suit ripped.

On another occasion, Safia gave a grand dinner for First Ladies at a luxurious revolving restaurant on the twenty-sixth floor of the Tripoli Tower. Around midnight, when the banquet was over, a stream of cars left the complex, which was located on the capital city's seafront, to take each one of the ladies back to her hotel. But one of the cars separated from the convoy. The driver had been ordered to split off as discreetly as possible toward Bab al-Azizia. Only one problem: no one at her hotel had been forewarned, and the delegation in charge of accompanying her was in an uproar, its chief of protocol almost apoplectic. "This is a disgrace!" he shouted at the Libyan organizers. "Where is Madame la Présidente? How could you lose the wife of a state leader in the middle of the night?" They tried to reassure him: security in Tripoli was omnipresent; this was merely a small glitch. Telephone in hand, he was panic-stricken, didn't know whom to alert, and was worried stiff. Having nothing to offer as an argument, the Libyan Department of Protocol thought it better to disappear. Faced with this situation they were confused but, at least, they didn't worry about her location. She returned at three-thirty in the morning.

I was told in great detail many more stories concerning the companions of state leaders, but also referring to female ministers from foreign countries, ambassadors, and heads of delegations. And even one story about a daughter of King Abdullah of Saudi Arabia. Gaddafi was ready to do anything to have this young woman; it would be an act of revenge, as he had had a serious conflict with her father who, at the time, was the only heir to the throne. A Lebanese go-between was given carte blanche to bring the young woman to him. But having failed to get to her, the wily go-between managed to convince a Moroccan woman who had lived in Saudi Arabia to pass for the princess, for just one single encounter and supported by a considerable sum of money. Betrayed by his arrogance and pride, the Colonel was fooled.

In the searching look of my interviewees I would, at times, sense the same concern I'd initially come across in Soraya: Will she believe me? Can she believe me? All of this is so larger-than-life! I would take notes without any comment, asking for details, for dates. She gave those to me, begging me not to reveal any names. Most of her stories were later confirmed to me by two other individuals, interpreters who worked in the same department and who were members of the group currently in power.

Finally, there was other prey, who were taboo and therefore all the more desirable for a man who took everything by right: the lovers and wives of his sons and cousins. There were innumerable rumors on this point. One rebel leader told me that his daughter-in-law, now living abroad, had personally confessed to him she was "repelled" by the mores of this "degenerate" family, and admitted that she had been forced to give in to the Guide's urgent advances a dozen times. I didn't dwell on this very much, as I saw it as yet another disgrace for a family about whom no one had any further illusions. But on February 28, 2012, the front page of the newspaper *Libya Al Jadida* announced an interview with Sayed Kadhaf Eddam, one of Gaddafi's closest cousins, which attracted my attention. In a country where the press had always been gagged and where the subject of sex continued to be taboo, the article was astounding.

Interviewed in prison and extremely bitter, Sayed Kadhaf Eddam condemned the brutal rape of his wife by his cousin Gaddafi. A rape, he said, that was premeditated, by a man who feared neither man nor God, and who when he desired a woman—or wanted to use her to "crush" her husband—"only had to make connections that united him with a clan, a tribe, or a family." Gaddafi raped his cousin's wife several times, he said, while he had been away from home on military missions, leading the woman, his "great love," to reject any link with the Gaddafi clan, quickly request a divorce, and hurriedly accept a position abroad. To save herself. And to protect their daughter, for she didn't want her family to "be struck by the same fate twice." The vocabulary was emotional and the tone surprisingly maudlin for a man known for escapades of all kinds and his closeness to the Guide. "He consumed her like a hot meal, until she reached the point of hating the fact that she was a woman."

So I made my way to the Al-Huda Prison in Misrata. The accusation was extremely serious, and as far as I know it was the first time that a man "of the family," whose ex-wife later pursued a diplomatic career at the United Nations by revealing herself to be a fierce defender of the Colonel, was risking himself in such a minefield. A few years earlier, the rage—for similar reasons—of another cousin of the Gaddafi tribe had ended with his terrifying public lynching.

The guards let me into Gaddafi's cousin's room in the prison's infirmary, a shambles of suitcases, cardboard boxes, books and medications, and a wheelchair. Enveloped in a brown djellaba, Eddam was receiving from his bed, lying on his side, one chubby hand supporting his head, wrapped in a turban with blue pompons, the other digging into a plate of dates and other dried fruit. Ill-shaven, a cunning expression on his face, and with a bulging belly, he reminded me of a weary, decadent pasha in an orientalist painting. Born in 1948, he looked ten years older than he was, and suffered from a partial paralysis. But he didn't look unhappy with his lot, insisting on being treated with respect and delighted that his incarceration had given him time to write his third novel. So I launched into the conversation by citing the interview in the Libyan newspaper, openly delighted that a man of the innermost circle, like himself, would contribute to having the truth emerge about the dictator's sexual crimes. Discomfort . . . He cleared his throat, shook his head to move a mischievous pompon that had escaped from the turban, and tried a solemn look. "That's a misunderstanding."

"Excuse me?"

"I never spoke of any sexual crime."

"Perhaps those are not the words you used, but you did describe Gaddafi's maneuvers to get you to be away while he forced your wife to—"

"My former wife was always faithful to me! My honor is secure!"

"She is not the issue. It is Gaddafi, whom you accused of—"

"Of nothing! I plan to bring charges to the paper that invented these things. I don't want history to connect me to this file! And one doesn't criticize the members of one's own family!"

He remained rigid. It was impossible to come back to the facts, so we circumvented them. For him, incriminating his cousin was out of the question: "You don't go digging through the graves of the dead. God alone can judge them." But he was so concerned with being exonerated of any complicity himself that he did have to express some strong reservations: "As an intellectual I couldn't approve of some of the activities." And then, a little later: "As a Bedouin, I felt he derided our values." Finally: "As a military man who, in 1979, established the Al-Saadi barracks, where my father is buried, I was horrified that he would tarnish the place by bringing all those women there. That disgusted me!"

The day after this conversation I rushed to the newspaper that had come out with the story of the rape. Sayed Kadhaf Eddam had, indeed, called from his prison, saying he and his family were humiliated and outraged by the article. But the editor in chief stuck by every word, stating that it only confirmed what all of Tripoli had already known for a long time. Furthermore, the follow-up to the interview was published in a different issue of the paper with, in the center of the page, a photo of Gaddafi's cousin speaking into the interviewer's tape recorder.

6

MANSOUR DAW

The only pictures available of him date to his capture on October 20, 2011, the same day that Muammar Gaddafi was captured. A short chaotic film taken by a rebel on a cell phone shows him haggard, disheveled, hair and beard unkempt, a wound caused by explosives beneath his right eye. His frantic flight with the Libyan Guide, whose much-feared chief of security he was, ended in carnage at the edge of the desert. This was the terrible image of a man defeated.

Mansour Daw stayed with the Libyan dictator until the very end, hurriedly leaving Bab al-Azizia when the insurgents seized Tripoli, first rushing off toward Bani Walid, where Gaddafi said farewell to his gathered family before heading for Sirte in the west—hiding there in ordinary houses that soon lacked all reserves, electricity, or food, and increasingly outnumbered

by rebels—until the ultimate attempt at flight was stopped
outright at dawn by NATO firing. Mansour was one of the few
survivors of the last group of the faithful. And together with
Gaddafi's son Saif al-Islam, he was the most important of the
prisoners captured by the new regime. His name embodied
the terror that was maintained for decades, and more recently
the barbarous acts—rape, torture, executions—committed in
his country to put down the revolution. All of Libya was waiting for him to explain himself. But Mansour Daw wasn't talking. At least, that is what Ibrahim Beitalmal, a member of the
Misrata Military Council and in charge of the military prisoners, was eager to warn me about when he gave me permission
to meet with him.

On Saturday, March 10, 2011, he came into the large meeting hall of a building of the national army in Misrata, looking relaxed—in a khaki jacket, a wool cap on his head—and
rested. His white beard was trimmed very short, and an ironic
smile played around his lips. He had agreed to the idea of an
interview without knowing its topic. Perhaps he saw it as a dis-
traction in his solitary days. "I was in France four times," he
said as an introduction. "It was very nice." All well and good,
but we weren't here to exchange pleasantries. I told him that I
was investigating a subject that was said to be taboo, the sexual
crimes of Colonel Gaddafi, and I was hoping he would tell me
what he knew about it. "Nothing," he answered. "I knew nothing. As a member of his family I owed him respect. So there
was no question of broaching the subject with him. Besides, I

didn't even let myself look in that direction. Keeping my distance was the best way for me to keep my self-respect. I was protecting myself."

"You knew, however, that Gaddafi was sexually abusing hundreds of young men and women?"

"I can't deny or confirm that. Everyone has the right to a private life."

"A private life? Can you talk about a private life when sexual relations are coerced, when there are countless accomplices, and state departments are called upon to facilitate these crimes?"

"Some people knew. I didn't."

"Did you know that young girls were held captive in the basement of his residence?"

"I swear I never went down to that basement! I am a commander and one of the highest-ranking officers in the army. In Moscow I wrote a thesis on military command structure. When I walk into a barracks, people tremble with fear. I've always known how to get respect—specifically, by keeping my distance from all that!"

"All that"? What did he mean? Suddenly he seemed ill at ease. Undoubtedly he was expecting to be faced with—and to dodge—questions about the war, arms, brigades, and mercenaries, but not questions about women. He was finding himself on shaky ground and was on his guard.

"What did the high command you personified think when you saw your leader disembark, surrounded by female bodyguards, most of whom were just young mistresses without any military training, to visit leaders of foreign countries?"

"I was not in charge of those trips and refused to participate in them! In the brief period of time that I myself ran the Guide's security brigade, I can assure you that the girls in that 'special service' weren't there!"

"Weren't you insulted by that masquerade?"

"What could I say? I didn't have a monopoly over the Libyan army! And even if I was unhappy, there was nothing I could do. In any event, women aren't made for the army. It goes against nature. If they'd asked for my opinion there never would have been a Military Academy for Women."

"Did Gaddafi genuinely believe in it when he created it in 1979?"

"Perhaps. But essentially I think that it is the academy that gave him the idea of using women in other ways."

He gave a little laugh as, with a trace of male complicity, he made eye contact with the prison director, who had just joined us, as if to say: "You know what I mean by 'using in other ways.'" So then I asked him if he knew the female bodyguards Soraya had told me about, Salma Milad in particular. I described her as being built like a tank, with a gun at her belt, watching over the Guide on every trip, ironing his clothes and tormenting his little slaves. He didn't hesitate. Of course, he had known her very well! He even acknowledged that she'd gained a certain level of competence at the Military Academy.

But the prominent place she had won by Gaddafi's side was still hard to swallow, even now. "That shocked me, you know. That display of closeness actually embarrassed me. Believe me, I even shouted against it. And when she was under my command I wouldn't let her get away with anything. One day when we were on a mission in Kufra, in the southern part of the country, I gave her an earful on the internal radio. Gaddafi intercepted the conversation and intervened, seething: 'Never talk to her like that again! One day I'll make her a general, you'll see. And she will be your superior!' My heart missed a beat. 'If you make her a general, she'll still never be anything but Salma Milad to me!' Every receiver linked to the network heard the exchange and Gaddafi was extremely offended by it. How could anyone speak to the head of the army that way? He had a plane pick me up and I did thirty days in solitary. So? What do you think of that? It shows you I have values, morals, that I draw the line."

Gradually, Mansour Daw let his guard down. Although I had been told that he didn't yet allow himself to be at all critical of the Guide, I sensed he was eager to clear himself of any involvement in the heinous business we were discussing. Strictly speaking, he revealed nothing, only hinted at things, but through these hints he confirmed that those close to Gaddafi were familiar with most of his activities, even participated in some of them, and tolerated no criticism. The leader's relations with women, military or not, was a private matter. Anyone who hindered him could count on his wrath. On the other hand, those who were willing to understand, encourage, and facilitate their master's sick obsession came to hold considerable power inside the regime. And Mansour Daw was unable to hide his contempt.

"How was this activity organized?"

"It fell under the umbrella of the Department of Protocol under the direction of Nuri Mesmari, a schemer who had the gall to parade around in a general's uniform every now and then, and had the nickname 'the general of special affairs' so the only word that was applicable could be avoided."

"And what was that?"

"I hardly dare tell you: 'general of the whores'! He looked for women everywhere; that was his specialty and his primary function; he would even pick up prostitutes on the street."

"And Mabrouka Sherif?"

"Crucial to the system. She actually carried a lot of weight with Gaddafi, and was glued to his side on a permanent basis. I was so revolted by her that I refused to shake her hand on three separate occasions. She had networks all over and dealt, among other things, with the wives of state leaders. She practiced black magic, and I'm sure that she used it to keep Gaddafi under her control."

"Did he believe in black magic?"

"He denied it, but although we're living in a scientific era, even Western leaders consult clairvoyants! In any case, there were several of us who wanted to tell him that Mabrouka Sherif and Mesmari practiced it. I remember one day when there were five of us high-ranking military officers in the car with him, I was driving, and one of us said: 'Watch out! You're the victim of black magic and those two are busy wrecking your image.' He shrugged his shoulders. 'I have complete confidence in them.' All my warnings failed completely. He was the head of state and I was nothing but a paid employee. I'm not the one who needs to answer for his crimes!"

"When did you work closely with the Department of Protocol?"

"Virtually never, for, as I told you, I would refuse to be part of the official trips Mesmari organized. But they still asked me to go to Spain, to France, et cetera. Even if they put my name on the list and reserved a room for me at the hotel, I'd refuse. I didn't want to be mixed up in that."

"Mixed up in what?"

"These goings-on with women."

"Because those trips were favorable for various forms of making deals?"

"I heard a lot of things, because there were clashes with the actual military. As chief of protocol, Mesmari, who spoke several languages, managed to disguise the arrivals of the women as 'committees,' 'delegations,' or 'groups of journalists.' I also know that this 'special service' was a very lucrative business for his officials, especially if they went abroad and tampered with the gifts. I knew how to protect myself."

Then I brought up Soraya's testimony. How Salma and Mabrouka kidnapped her in Sirte, her successive rapes, her incarceration in a basement at Bab al-Azizia. He shook his head, devastated. "I wasn't consulted on that sort of subject. I could have opposed it. They would have put me in prison. I swear I knew nothing about that basement! It goes against my values! I am a respected military man, a father, a grandfather. Can you see me as a rapist? A pimp? Never! I'd be incapable of sleeping with a woman who isn't interested!" There was a moment of silence during which he seemed lost in his thoughts. He took a deep breath, threw a meaningful look at the two rebels in charge of the prison, and, raising his arms to the sky, exclaimed: "He who should have been the nation's spiritual leader! It's awful!"

Was he really surprised or was he putting on an act? Was it conceivable that Libya's chief of security was really dumbfounded as he heard mention of the crimes perpetrated by the master of Bab al-Azizia, while so many employees—guards, chauffeurs, nurses—were aware of them? "I didn't spend much time with him. We weren't close. We were closely related, and I stayed with him until the end. I even supported him when he was wounded, to bring him to safety. But I swear that this information comes as a shock! What I heard about the gynecological examination room at the university gives me goose bumps."

"Would you say that sex was used as a political weapon?"

"Come now! That's a classic. You know very well that sex is used as a weapon all over the world. Even in France. The first time I went there I knew that the French Secret Service had signed up a Tunisian woman to trap me. Fair enough, but it showed how little they knew me. They don't pursue me—I am the one who pursues! Gaddafi often sent girls also to trap those close to him or highly placed people in the government. Some came to their downfall that way."

"Did you know that he forced some ministers to have sexual relations with him?"

"It doesn't surprise me. There are so many ambitious people. There were even those who were prepared to hand over their wife or daughter in exchange for some favor or other. That is the height of disgrace in Libyan culture. It's the sign of a subhuman."

"Apparently, he also tried to rape the wives of his cousins."

"You're not a man if you allow your own wife to be touched."

"How should you react?"

"By killing the rapist. Or by bringing about your own death."

"You can't be ignorant of the fact that he also assaulted wives of the guards and the military?"

"I guarantee you that he never touched my own family. I always did everything to protect them."

"How?"

"I made sure my wife never got into any car that wasn't driven by me or one of my sons. We didn't have a chauffeur. Except occasionally when I'd rely on the services of my wife's brother, who was even more protective than I was. And jealous, too!"

237

"So you didn't trust Gaddafi?"

"We didn't invite him to my son's wedding. On the third day Safia came to congratulate us and have her picture taken with my son and his wife. That was all."

"Why?"

"I didn't want my highly respected family to fall victim to his activities. The wedding was held at my house because I was afraid of the cameras at the hotels. The orchestra was made up of women, and the reception was all women except for my son. And we had prohibited any cell phones so that no pictures could be taken on the sly."

"Did you think he might have picked out a victim had he been invited to the reception?"

"He wouldn't have dared to pounce on any of my guests. He knew all too well what my reaction would have been. But I preferred that he be somewhere else. Had he come he would surely have been accompanied by his whores, always on the lookout, and that terrified me."

What an admission! What mistrust! Did he have any regrets for having followed such a shameless criminal all the way to the end? He sat up in his chair and took his time before answering.

"In the beginning I trusted him and had no idea about his barbaric acts. Now that he is dead, what's the point of expressing any personal regrets? I keep that to myself, buried deep inside me. I protected my family, and that to me is what's most important. And from here on in I surrender myself to the justice of the Libyan people. I will accept its verdict. Even if it's a death sentence."

He got up to leave, waiting to be taken back to his cell, then changed his mind.

"You know, when I came here, to Misrata, this city that had been so badly damaged by the war, I had lost a great deal of blood. I was wounded, on the brink of death. They took care of me and treated me with respect. I need to say that. I sleep on a mattress that the prison director brought me himself from his own home. He gave me clothes. I'm discovering the pleasure of speaking with good men, who fought for the rebellion, and the almost fraternal link that unites us. Unsettling, isn't it?"

7

ACCOMPLICES AND
PROVIDERS

Back to Tripoli, that strange city, both modern and out-moded, clogged and chaotic, distorted, not knowing what it is anymore. Maybe it has a hidden charm. Within the maze of its enclosed medina you will, no doubt, find souks and great sculpted wooden doors, opulent mosques, and secret palaces. Some of the centrally located districts still have some attractive remnants of the Italian era, and the Square of the Martyrs is a place where children can run and play in the open air. But in the particularly humid and cool winter of 2012, I was not exactly sensitive to the appeal of this odd capital city that borders the Mediterranean without deigning to look out toward it.

I crisscrossed the city in dilapidated black and white taxi-cabs with cracked windshields, and often with at least one door that wouldn't open. One driver I was with on a memorable journey couldn't have cared less. He took off enthusiastically to confront traffic jams on roads full of potholes, ignoring traffic lights or who had the right-of-way, humming the revolutionary songs the radio belched out, without ever admitting that he didn't know the address I had given him. "Yallah, let's go!" He improvised a concert of honking, suddenly stopped to ask directions, then backtracked repeatedly, yelling *Merci, Sarkozy!*" when he found out with glee that I was French. I smiled and mimicked his V for Victory. NATO's intervention in support of the revolution deserved eternal gratitude, he said. It was a time of optimism.

However, the winter was rough for the inhabitants of Tripoli. Most of the public and private construction sites were at a standstill—motionless cranes stood outlined against the sky like mournful wading birds. Many of the economic sectors, completely in ruins, had let go of hordes of workers, who were now wandering through the streets, covered in filth, looking to hustle or for a bit of work as they awaited better days. The rebels were deferring the departure of their brigades, nostalgic for the more dangerous times that had bound them together, still intoxicated with the victory, ready for a fight with a rival militia, shaky about their future, unable to plan for the short term. Voices were being raised ever louder decrying the lack of transparency of the new power, the National Transitional Council, whose membership list had never been made public, and condemning the inefficiency of the temporary government. People talked of vague attempts at separatism in the east, intertribal conflicts in the south, and pockets of pro-Gaddafi resistance in the west. But in Tripoli, where bulldozers had razed the Bab al-Azizia compound to the ground with the intention of one day transforming it into a huge public park, time seemed to hang suspended. It was a city without any direction. And my interviewees were up against it.

When I would call on some of the people whose names had been given to me, the first reaction was close to panic: "How did you get my name? From whom? Why? I have nothing to do with that subject, you hear? Don't ever quote me! You have no right to destroy my life!" Sometimes the panic would turn to anger and threats would follow, but usually these outbursts died down; explanation, moderation, reassurance, and the promise of secrecy were needed. But countless appointments I had gone to great effort to arrange were canceled, postponed, or put off indefinitely without any explanation. One commander who was supposed to drive me to a key witness suddenly stopped answering his cell phone. I was eventually told he'd been taken to a hospital in Tripoli, then to a different place in Tunis, where he died. It's possible. How would one know? Another person I'd been in touch with suddenly was "away on a trip." Another one "fell ill." I couldn't get used to it.

The tracks Soraya had steered me onto all turned out to be the right ones: abductions, incarcerations, rapes, the masquerade of bodyguards, and the permanent flow of women and young men to the bedroom of a sick and brutality-obsessed dictator. What remained to be better understood was how Gaddafi's networks functioned, how over the course of so many years he was guaranteed a daily supply of fresh meat. Of course, he had accomplices everywhere, men who shared his tastes and knew it was the surest way to acquire his gratitude as well as various other advantages, including receiving women in return. And once the women themselves had passed through his bed, they understood that by skillfully placating the Guide, they could grow considerably richer: at least one became a woman minister, others female police agents, teachers, bankers, hairdressers; still others found work in hotels or in the luxury sector, in tourism or business.

But some intermediaries close to Gaddafi were especially efficient. Over the course of my interviews the names of two men in particular kept cropping up: Abdallah Mansour (former chief of interior intelligence, especially close to the Guide) and Ali al-Kilani, both of whom had an army background, were said to be poets and songwriters, had worked as artists' agents and producers, and, first one and then the other, directed the General Office of Libyan Radio and Television, a powerful propaganda tool. Their relationships with people in show business gave them access to dozens of young and naïve people who dreamed of working in television and theater. Every casting session provided new prey, as did each interview in cafés and hotels, where the two men behaved like gentlemen before acting like boors.

They also had every conceivable and desirable contact with female singers, dancers, and actresses in the Mediterranean region and would find a thousand pretexts to invite them to the Guide's home or to beautiful villas, where the women would organize meetings and huge parties. Gaddafi had noticed the young hostess of a children's program on the Arab MBC station? Abdallah Mansour would contact her channel's management and invite her to Libya to organize an event in "homage" to her incredible talent. A Lebanese journalist had attracted his attention? The two men would attempt to get her to come to Libya, even if they had to create the funding for a bogus production company for a phony artistic project to make her do so. Enormous sums (up to millions of euros) might be spent on wooing a woman like this, and a private jet put at her disposal. Mansour and Kilani had connections in many Arab countries—in Morocco, Tunisia, Egypt, Jordan, and Lebanon. There were countless commissions and substantial rewards if the Guide declared he was satisfied with their service.

On every visit to an African country Gaddafi relied on the services of his diplomats and a few local figures to arrange for him to meet with women's associations and groups. This would guarantee sustaining his reputation as the hero of the women's cause, since he could portray the entire visit as being of a political or religious character (as with the feast of Mouloud he celebrated in Timbuktu in 2006 and in Agades in 2007).

It was above all an opportunity to make devoted "women friends" there, whom he provided with generous subsidies, in addition to necklaces and medallions with his image. It was their task to turn into attentive intermediaries, responsible for organizing his next welcoming committee—which he liked to be exultant, bursting with admiration, and resplendent; and not only at conferences, parties, festivals, and parades, but at baptisms and weddings, they would be expected to spot new young girls to be invited to Libya. Yes, indeed: "to be invited." It was as simple as that. In the "brother countries" Gaddafi had the reputation of being rich, splendid, and generous. The suitcases full of banknotes brought to his suite were as famous— and as anticipated—as his anti-American diatribes and his eccentric garb.

Thus, everyone found it perfectly normal that he was generous with invitations to come see him in Libya. Wasn't he selling Libya as a kind of "paradise for women"? One young Libyan woman educated in Niamey, Niger, told me that in the cafés and nightclubs of the capital cities of Mali or Niger, she frequently ran into groups of young girls excited about going to Libya the next day. "They weren't hiding it, but were loudly proclaiming their luck. 'Papa Muammar,' they'd say, 'wanted so much to please the girls that he invited them, all expenses paid, to spend their vacation in his country. Isn't he the most thoughtful of all men?'"

These voyages of discovery were reported to me by Fatma. A friend from the Tuareg ethnic group had phoned her and she agreed to meet me without any conditions. After so many refusals, I was grateful to her. Slender, her head held high and her gait relaxed, she came smiling broadly into the foyer of the Corinthia, a luxury hotel, where the little gestures she made for all to see soon told me she knew the whole staff and was a regular there. An icy storm was sweeping through the city but she was draped in diaphanous veils and pretty shoes that bared her ankles. She was thirty-six years old and said she was a Mauritanian from Niger but had been in Libya for twenty months. Thanks to Muammar Gaddafi. How had that happened? She burst out laughing. "Oh, very simply!" A Nigerian woman friend married to a Tuareg who knew Mabrouka had suggested one day in 2003 that she come to visit Tripoli with four other girls. "It was a tempting offer: airplane, visits, four-star hotels, everything provided by the Libyan state! And spending money too! What would you have done in my place? You would have said yes right away, and happily so!" I was thrilled that she replied for me because my answer would not have been so enthusiastic.

She continued. The invitation was such a gift, and a few weeks later she landed at Tripoli Airport together with four delighted companions. Jalal (employed in the group of Gaddafi's boys and fleetingly in love with Soraya) was waiting to escort them to the Al Mehari Hotel (a five-star hotel long under the direction of Nuri Mesmari). They were given an envelope with five hundred dinars so they could do some shopping before their program of tourism and visits began. After a few days the group was told to get dressed to visit "Papa." A car from Bab al-Azizia came to pick them up at the hotel, followed by a car with Gaddafi guards, which Fatma explained "proved to us that we were important guests." Mabrouka received them and brought them to a series of reception rooms. Then Gaddafi appeared in a "very simple" red jogging suit. He showed an interest in each one of them, inquiring after their names, families, tribes, languages, leisure activities. "You like Libya? Oh, how I wish that everyone would be so crazy about my country!"

Fatma remembered how "sweet" and how "funny" he was. At one point he even turned to Mabrouka and said: "It would be good to have Fatma work for us. I see she speaks Arabic, Tuareg, Songhai, French . . . That would be extremely valuable to us!" According to Fatma, Mabrouka seemed annoyed and jealous but she agreed. The small group went back to the hotel on a cloud. "That someone like he would be interested in us in such a personal way was really flattering." Wasn't it?

The "vacation" lasted two or three weeks. Jalal and the chauffeur were at their beck and call and more gifts came their way. Fatma confirmed she didn't see Gaddafi again before her departure, but she soon returned to Tripoli. She was accompanied by other young women, one of whom was a little Malian bombshell, a flamboyant, spoiled jet-setter who'd been noticed previously by Nuri Mesmari, who once before had sent a private jet to bring her to Gaddafi. "Her skintight clothes and her low-cut tank tops caused us problems in the street but Gaddafi loved it! He was crazy about her and regularly called for her. I would wait, together with Mabrouka. As he came out of his bedroom Gaddafi would say, 'Take good care of my guests,' which meant: 'Don't forget the presents and the money.'" During their various stays, Jalal gave them Rado, Tissot, or other brands of watches, bracelets, and earrings, top Italian name pendants, and necklaces with a photo of the Guide framed in diamonds—and then, just before they'd catch their plane, an envelope containing varying sums of money, ranging from two thousand to twenty thousand dollars, "depending on the guests I had brought."

Of course, Fatma omitted some crucial details concerning her role. She dodged some questions, laughing and feigning sincerity: "That's how we are, we Mauritanians! We have a talent for PR and commerce!" This seemed to me to correspond quite nicely with the job of a matchmaker or courtesan. She also said, without offering any further details: "We Mauritanians don't like being ordered around and choose our men ourselves rather than being chosen by them." In any case, it seems she had brought the Guide streams of women from different countries—"the last time, seventeen who came from Nouakchott [the capital of Mauritania] for the feast of Mouloud"—and since everyone knew of her links with Bab al-Azizia, she also served as an intermediary with ministers, ambassadors, and contractors from African countries. "Mabrouka dealt with the wives and daughters of presidents who wanted to see Gaddafi. My terrain was much wider!"

But, she insisted, the Guide's generosity toward women was boundless, recalling that the luxury hotels in Tripoli, the best of which was the Mehari, were forever occupied by these idle guests from far and wide, waiting for their appointments. It was equally clear that Fatma had become very close to the dictator. On various occasions she had accompanied him to Benghazi and Sirte as well as on his jaunts into the desert; she had attended the ceremonies of national holidays, rubbed elbows with Safia and daughters Aisha and Hana, the latter "always trailing behind her older sister." Such good memories, she said.

And very good business.

The Bab al-Azizia drivers were in an ideal position to assist in the innumerable comings and goings of women. One of them, Hussein, who worked for the Department of Protocol, spoke to me of his endless commutes between the Mehari and the airport to transport young girls. They arrived from all over, he said: from other cities in Libya but also from Lebanon, Iraq, the Gulf states, Bosnia, Serbia, Belgium, Italy, France, and the Ukraine. As a rule, they were all about twenty years old, beautiful "even without makeup," and long-haired. Someone from protocol was in charge of welcoming them, and then they were brought directly to the hotel, where they'd be for several hours or several days until—more often than not around one o'clock in the morning—Hussein came to pick them up and drive them to Bab al-Azizia. "I would wait quietly in the parking lot there. Around five the girl would knock on my window and I'd take her back to the hotel, always followed by a car with guards."

Some of them would come out happy, others were distraught. Some left the next day, while others would be called back several nights in a row. They all arrived with minimal baggage, but the majority would depart with several suitcases. And in his rearview mirror Hussein would see wads of banknotes. "I swear it on the head of my son: one of them pulled out a hundred-dollar bill from her Samsonite suitcase—which was overflowing with cash—rolled it up, and snorted cocaine from it. One hundred dollars! More than a month's salary for me!" Another one, a famous Lebanese singer who had spent the night with Gaddafi, was given instructions to withdraw a million euros from a bank in five-hundred-euro bills. "Completely disgusted at that point, I decided to quit my job. I thought Gaddafi had prestige. He was nothing but disgraceful." One of Hussein's colleagues, responsible for picking up the girls from the Corinthia Hotel, stated that on several occasions a Ukrainian nurse was sent to the hotel to publicly take blood from him to prove to the girls who'd been picked to go to Bab al-Azizia and were concerned about this odd procedure that it was done to everyone, without distinction.

Muammar Gaddafi's well-known obsession with women sometimes aroused the ire of foreign politicians. A minister of foreign affairs from Senegal indignantly reported that he had firmly refused to leave the only woman among his coworkers behind in Tripoli, as the Guide had stipulated, while the rest of the delegation was leaving. Another minister had demanded an explanation—which was not provided—when he caught wind of an AIDS screening test systematically done on young Malian women invited to a hotel. Another visitor said he had intercepted photographs that emissaries of the Guide had circulated in order to find some girls he had seen during a visit to Niger. Someone else had initiated an investigation, one that was rapidly suppressed, when he learned that some girls who'd been "invited" by the Guide had had their passports confiscated and felt "sequestered" at the Mehari Hotel. One day, Nuri Mesmari's frantic efforts to entice the Guide by always making more and more lovely women available to him actually caused a diplomatic scandal between Libya and Senegal.

On September 1, 2001, a parade of hundreds of fashion models from all over Africa were supposed to celebrate the thirty-second anniversary of Colonel Gaddafi's coming to power. Of course, gifted with great sums of money, the Libyan embassies in various countries were expected to contribute women, activating all their contacts in the fashion world, as well as rounding up call girls. In Senegal, the task of recruiting girls had been entrusted to the twin daughters of a Senegalese actor, Nancy and Leila Campbell, who were already working for Gaddafi, and who were especially careless, since at the end of one casting call, which was held both in the street and with a celebrated stylist, they made an appointment for August 28 at the Dakar airport with roughly a hundred young women,

who'd been invited to spend a week in Tripoli. Tall, slim, lav-
ishly dressed, and full of hope, the women were there, lined up
at seven in the morning, ready to board the plane. The chargé
d'affaires of the Libyan Embassy made sure they were well
received and a Boeing 727, chartered in Malta, was waiting for
them on the tarmac.

But not long before takeoff, police and security personnel
at Léopold Sédar Senghor Airport, intrigued by the special
nature of the "cargo" and the lack of tickets and visas for the
passengers, some of whom were minors, alerted the authorities and kept the plane from leaving. Unprepared for this, the
Senegalese government reacted sharply and immediately condemned the Libyans' plan as an attempt at "extracting" young
Senegalese girls. The Senegalese minister of foreign affairs,
Cheikh Tidiane Gadio, was outraged and said the affair
revealed Libyan diplomacy as "unacceptable and unfriendly,"
adding that Senegal was not an "open-door state." A few hours
later, the Senegalese minister of the interior, General Mama-
dou Niang, declared in a communiqué that the girls Libya was
trying to "extract" from the national territory were destined to
become part of an international prostitution ring and that he
was going to Interpol with this.

At that point, the newspapers went wild. "Attempt to
extract young Senegalese women; the state questions Libya,"
was a headline in the *Sud Quotidien* of August 30, 2001.
Indeed, the Senegalese ambassador in Tripoli was called back
to Dakar for consultation. A Libyan delegation was sent to

Senegal to meet with the ministers of foreign affairs and of culture. The Senegalese president, Abdoulaye Wade, officially declared he felt "wounded." In his fury he even called Gaddafi, and it took a myriad of promises and all the diplomacy one of his collaborators—who told me about this event—could muster to avoid a diplomatic breakdown and repair the damage.

Models were, of course, part of the dictator's fantasy world. In a country where at least 95 percent of the women are veiled, he was forever organizing fashion shows during parties, festivals, and even political summits. Alphadi, the fashion designer from Niger known as the "Magician of the Desert" and thought of as the standard-bearer of African fashion, expressed his eternal gratitude to him. "Ah, I can truly say that Gaddafi supported me!" he told me. "He gave me lots of money, sent planes for me, subsidized my shows! He had such faith in Africa. And such a commitment to serving his country, and especially to fashion." Sincere, really? "Completely! You should know how much he helped me launch the first International Festival of African Fashion [held in Niger in 1998], and subsequently known throughout the world. He sent ministers and fashion models from his own country. I could ask him for anything!" Anything. The joy Gaddafi felt in meeting top models was worth any number of subsidies and advantages to the creator from Niger.

"But, for God's sake, Mr. Alphadi, didn't you know the Guide was a predator?"

"There were rumors to that effect about him and his entourage. Libyans are great skirt chasers. I was aware of the risks. But I wasn't involved in prostitution. And before a show in Sirte, for instance, I gathered my girls and told them: 'Watch out, stay together in a group, and count your numbers. Don't go out alone!' Thank God, I always brought them all back home with me."

However, nothing, certainly not fine principles, could put the brakes on the dictator's insatiable appetite. In November 2009, his ever-resourceful chief of protocol contacted Hostessweb, an Italian agency of hostesses (with the protocol man's sister as intermediary). Outside a conference of the FAO (the Food and Agricultural Organization of the United Nations) on world hunger in Rome, the chief said, Gaddafi wanted to address a female audience. Alerted at the very last minute, the agency let it be known via SMS and the Internet that it was looking for attractive young women, at least five-feet-eight, well dressed, and in high heels but not miniskirts or plunging necklines. Two hundred women showed up for the appointment at a fine hotel, thinking they'd be playing bit parts at a meeting and then a cocktail hour, since they were being paid only about sixty euros for the evening. None of them could have guessed at that point that the buses would take them to the residence of the Libyan ambassador, where, to their utter surprise, Muammar Gaddafi, in a white limousine, joined them to give them a long speech . . . on Islam, the religion "that is not against women." It was a rambling speech by which he expected to motivate conversion and rectify some untruths: "You believe that Jesus was crucified but that isn't true—God brought him to heaven. They crucified someone who resembled him." The young women left with the Koran and the *Green Book* in hand.

The Italian press and some politicians were upset by this event and questioned the dictator's actual intentions. But Alessandro Londero, Hostessweb's director, was ready to defend the Guide. None of the girls had spent the night at his residence; Londero had counted and recounted them. It simply concerned an "evening of a passionate discussion on religion and Libyan culture." A discussion? "But of course," Londero insisted when I reached him by phone in Rome. "The Guide sensed that there was incomprehension and a lack of knowledge about his country. So there was just one thing he wished for: to bring the cultures closer together and establish a dialogue between the young people of Libya and the West. He asked the audience for their questions and answered them patiently and in an edifying manner. I can assure you that it was a unique experience for all those young girls!" Islam? "Oh, he was clever! He didn't expect, of course, that his call to a conversion to Islam would draw a crowd of people ready to convert. But he knew that the media impact would be enormous."

In fact, the experiment was repeated, and over no fewer than four evenings more than a thousand pretty girls—the director insisted on telling me there were also a few boys and some "normal" girls in attendance—served as the dictator's docile audience. A very small number said they were ready to embrace Islam and provided their telephone numbers, which were quickly noted down by a staff member at the ready. But the Guide didn't stop at that. Solid connections were made with the modeling agency, which was then allowed to organize a dozen or so trips to Libya for groups ranging from twelve to twenty-four people—all expenses paid, the stays intended to "deepen their ties to Libyan culture and lifestyle." It was a marvelous vacation, one of the girls, an Anglo-Italian actress, later told me. She was thrilled to have shared the Guide's breakfast (camel's milk and dates) during a jaunt into the desert, and became convinced that "women are treated better in Libya than anywhere else."

Some of the girls were swayed to such a degree that they would later participate in demonstrations in Rome against the NATO strikes, and that a small group of them, led by Londero, would go to Tripoli in August 2011, at the agency director's own expense, to demonstrate their support while braving the bombs. It was a sojourn from which Alessandro Londero returned in a state of shock, bringing with him a letter of appeal for help from Gaddafi to Berlusconi, written on August 5, just before his hasty departure from Bab al-Azizia, a letter that Abdallah Mansour had entrusted to Londero. Thus the director of a fashion modeling agency became the final messenger of a dictator on the run. Just a short line in the book of history, no doubt.

8

MABROUKA

Since my first meeting with Soraya in the fall of 2011, I had been obsessed by one name: Mabrouka. I wasn't familiar with its sound, even though I knew that in Arabic "Mabrouk" stands for "blessed" or "fortunate" and is often used to celebrate an event and start off a series of congratulatory wishes. But Soraya's "Mabrouka" had nothing cheerful to offer. Soraya's solemn voice uttered her name with such harshness, her eyes still haunted by memories she knew were impossible to share, that I associated it with the darkest of colors and a sense of evil incarnate. Who could she be, this woman who was prepared to commit any crime to satisfy her master, a complete madman? What sort of a relationship did she have with him? Was she doing her job under duress or was she fascinated, in his thrall? Was she motivated by ambition and a thirst for wealth and power, or were there maybe more complex and darker impulses in her zeal to anticipate the dictator's desires, fantasies, and perversions? Was she covering up personal humiliations and a secret wound? Was she taking revenge? What had her life been like before Bab al-Azizia?

Soraya knew nothing, or too little, to help me with this question. Mabrouka had been her abductor, her jailer, her torturer. She had wrecked her life, knowingly and irreversibly, and in five years had never shown the slightest sign of humanity or compassion. She was clearly not ignorant of the rapes, in fact facilitated them. She knew of the insults, the abuses, the savagery; she was a witness to, and a participant in, them. She was, as a Gaddafi collaborator told me later, "the mother madam in all her horror." And no one had any doubt that on occasion she was also Gaddafi's mistress. But one had to live within the proximity of the Guide to know this. For outside Bab al-Azizia, Mabrouka put on airs, passed herself off as one of the closest of the Colonel's advisers, fooling quite a few diplomats.

It took me a while to find her in the official photographs. She often stood in the Guide's shadow when he'd set foot on the red carpet rolled out for him on the runway of some foreign airport. She left the place of honor to the luscious Amazons but would monitor the scene with her rapacious eye, staying slightly in the background behind a sober black veil. She wore her brown hair tied back, her features were unremarkable, she never wore any makeup, she had a stern mouth, and she seemed drab and dull to me. But one European ambassador told me that she wasn't—badly dressed, "badly put together," yes; without any ostensible sign of coquetry or luxury; and "never in a mode of seduction." But he thought that she must have been beautiful when she was younger and that some of that beauty was still left. He figured she was about fifty years old.

Many heads of state, ministers, and diplomats had come across her during an official trip, an African summit, or an international conference. European and French people—Cécilia Sarkozy among them—had been in contact with her during the long negotiations over the liberation of some Bulgarian nurses, whom the Libyans had wrongly accused of vaccinating children with the AIDS virus. She was presented as the person in charge of protocol but everyone knew of her closeness, not to say intimacy, with Gaddafi. Obviously, she had his ear, and so they used her to get messages to him. Besides, she did everything to show that her power surpassed the perimeters of protocol, that she was "the woman who had the Guide's trust," that she could intercede in nominating ambassadors or other public officials, and that her role was increasingly a political one. Indeed, she occasionally phoned the diplomatic cell at the Elysée Palace to ask for a clarification of French policy in, say, Mali or Niger. She was also thought to be influential with the Tuaregs, whose leaders in Libya she knew, as well as those in neighboring countries such as Algeria, Mali, Niger, and Mauritania. No need, then, to state that they treated her with respect, even if a note from the French secret service, which had followed her during her Parisian trips, presented her as a "procurer" and one ambassador told me coldly: "She came to do her shopping." Shopping? "She was collecting girls to be sent to the Guide." Yes, indeed. She'd go to luxury hotels in the Champs-Elysées area—taking a suite at Fouquet's—and with phenomenal self-assurance would use every contact she had. At a reception one day she ran into Caroline Sarkozy, the president's half sister. Later that day, Mabrouka burst into her office, together with her interpreter and the driver at the Libyan Embassy, to ask her to sign a copy of her book on interior design to the Guide thusly: "To our brother Guide. I hope that you will enjoy this book on the beautiful homes of Paris." (The rebels found this book in August 2011 when they penetrated the luxurious Tripoli villa compound of Aisha.) Of course, Mabrouka's idea was to attract this lovely woman to the capital of Libya one day. If she knew that this or that princess from an Arab court—Saudi Arabia, Qatar—was in Paris, she would immediately make an appointment with her at the Ritz Hotel or the Four Seasons. Once she met the French minister of justice, Rachida Dati, who had North African roots, and asked to see her again at Fouquet's. She would draw up a list of female ministers and other influential women, primarily of Muslim background, and go from one appointment to the next. She'd phone Salma and say: "Ask brother Guide to make some money available for Princess X." Or: "Send me a case of pendants for the wives of some ambassadors." She'd make a short visit to Sephora to purchase perfumes the harem had ordered and would call Salma again to find out what the Guide needed. Powder, foundation, MAC Concealer? "It's for a middle-aged man," she'd specify to the salesman. "A gentleman like yourself." The young man couldn't have imagined in a million years that the beneficiary of these creams was Gaddafi, which made her interpreter laugh.

She also would take the time to hang around in certain luxury stores, fancy restaurants, or cafés in order to find pretty women and start a conversation. Her preference was for young girls from the Maghreb or the Gulf states whom she could address in Arabic. For the others she used the services of a translator, who was extremely smooth in his approach. "Do you know Libya? Oh, that's a country you should discover! Would you like to visit it? I can invite you there. I can even arrange a meeting for you with our Guide!" She would have her photograph taken with her potential prey, whose address she'd take down. She was on a constant hunt, with unlimited means. I was told another story of a young Moroccan woman whom Mabrouka had approached in a hotel, begging her to accept an invitation to Libya. After demanding that her cousin travel with her, the woman returned to France with fifty thousand dollars.

One night in Tripoli, a Tuareg chief who had known Mabrouka in her youth agreed to provide me with a few indispensable clues to her character. We were in a restaurant near the Old City and I planned to treat myself to a couscous with camel's meat. The chief was a man with the manners and healthy appearance of an aristocrat, equally comfortable in well-tailored jeans and cashmere jacket as in a white *gandoura*—a long, loose gown—and head covering. Even before I got out my notebook he took my arm and, staring at me, declared in a calm and serious voice: "She is a she-devil." He kept quiet for a time, as if to underline the impact of his words, and then went on: "She is the embodiment of evil and frighteningly skillful. There's nothing she wouldn't undertake to reach her goal: lies, schemes, betrayal, corruption, black magic. She is totally fearless, moves like a snake, and could 'put the wind in a bag and sell it to people.'"

Her father—of the Sherif family—came from Tuareg nobility but had married beneath his station after falling in love with a woman of a lower class who lived in the town of Ghat, in southern Libya, close to the Algerian border and not far from Niger. The couple had two daughters, Mabrouka and her older sister, whom they gave to slaves to be raised. This is a tradition, the chief explained to me, to ward off fate and "counteract the evil spirit" when parents have previously lost young children.

At a very young age Mabrouka was promised to an aristocratic Tuareg of Gaddafi's tribe. Already married to one of the Guide's cousins, this Massoud Abdel Hafiz suddenly married her. He was commander of the military region of Sebha, and for a brief moment Mabrouka was able to take advantage of the many privileges granted to those close to Gaddafi, and thus became fond of traveling in opulent style. But this high-ranking officer soon divorced her and she went back to live in Ghat, her birthplace. In contrast to most Tuareg women, she didn't wear traditional clothing and dressed Western style— "but without any taste," the chief added. She was said to have had a romance with a bank owner, and then she vanished, "gone up to Tripoli." He didn't know the precise circumstances of this narrow escape.

I would find out how Mabrouka had made it to Tripoli from someone in the Department of Protocol. Mabrouka had been hired there in 1999, on the occasion of a conference of African leaders, to which Gaddafi wanted to give a historic scope and luster, and where the famous "Sirte Declaration" was signed on September 9, 1999 (9-9-99), setting the objective of the Organization of African Unity. About thirty heads of state participated, which meant almost as many wives who needed to be received at the airport, accompanied to the places they went (hairdresser, shops, conferences), and provided with interpreters. Overwhelmed by the task, the Department of Protocol was obliged to quickly recruit women who could speak all kinds of African languages and dialects.

Knowing Tuareg and Haussa (a language spoken in Niger and Nigeria), Mabrouka came in through this crack in the door and thus penetrated the circle of power. "However, she didn't seem like anything special!" the person who had recruited her recalled. "She looked like a backward peasant girl, without any flirtatiousness or sophistication, probably very poor. In any event, that's what I thought. But she had such eagerness in her eyes!" A quick apprenticeship brought the newly hired together for advice and instruction on their role, their language, and their appearance (a modern suit was recommended). On the first day of the conference Mabrouka made her entrance at Bab al-Azizia, accompanying the delegation from Guinea that had come to greet Gaddafi. And that was it. That same evening she told her supervisor: "You have to find someone to replace me. Starting today, I work directly for the brother Guide." She had made it.

Later on, the family that had received her when she arrived in Tripoli reported how ardently she'd tried to find work and, above all, how stubbornly she'd insisted on meeting Gaddafi. "It would just take one time, she'd say. One time only! And he will want me in his service!" They all explained her success as coming from her intensive practice of black magic. Throughout her many years of service to Gaddafi, she met with the greatest sorcerers of Africa in their various countries, and had them invited to Tripoli.

So, gradually she became the sovereign lady of a kind of harem housed in the basement of the Guide's residence, where young girls were brought together as captives, where they ended up staying for years, trapped and incapable of being reintegrated into Libyan society. But she was also the authorized source of the kind of big game Gaddafi was looking for (I was told about her way of appreciating the musculature of very young men in Africa before sending them off to Gaddafi).

And lastly, she was the director of the "special service," those girls in uniform who supposedly made up the personal, flamboyant guard of the dictator. Woe to anyone who attracted her attention or accidentally mentioned a niece, a female cousin, a neighbor, or to anyone who came to Bab al-Azizia to ask for a favor (lodging, work, health care). Mabrouka was always waiting for an opportunity to throw out her nets.

"That woman was a disgrace to the Tuareg nation," one of its chiefs told me. "We all knew what that 'special service' signified. Did she benefit from her situation to target our women? She is capable of anything. But a Tuareg woman would rather kill herself than admit to having experienced anything of that nature."

I tried, of course, to find out where Mabrouka was. Early in the winter of 2011 they told me she had fled, as had the majority of those close to Gaddafi, and that she was in Algeria. Someone thought he'd seen her in Tunisia. Then I learned that she had mobilized a large number of people, notably among the Tuaregs, to try to convince the Algerian authorities to grant her political asylum. This request was refused. Early in March 2012, I learned that she had "negotiated" her return to Libyan soil and since then had been under house arrest in Ghat, living with her mother. In spite of my persistence, meeting her proved to be impossible. But to my great surprise, Ottman Mekta, the impressive rebel leader of Zintan who had interrogated her for three long days, showed her some leniency: "She expressed many regrets and even asked to be pardoned," he told me. "She stated she wasn't acting from her own free will and that, at the time, nobody was free! I saw that she was extremely attached to her elderly mother and I had the impression she was basically a good person who had been burdened with far too great a role."

A good person . . . I couldn't believe my ears. Was it possible she'd managed to change the opinion of her jailers? Should I share Soraya's testimony with them?

9

A MILITARY WEAPON

Writing an article that no one really wants to read is a frequent occurrence. After all, that is what the work of journalists consists of: working on upsetting topics, coming out with upsetting information, bringing out truths that cause anger. "Our profession is not meant to please, nor to do harm; it is meant to put one's finger on the problem," as Albert Londres, the tutelary figure of great Francophone reporters, wrote. Still, I didn't think I was writing a book that nobody in Libya would want anything to do with.

In the course of my investigation my few Libyan friends, supporters of this project, were insulted and threatened. And in the highest circles of the State they spoke of an "affront." If the rape of a young girl brings dishonor upon her entire family, particularly on its men, then the rape of thousands of women perpetrated by the country's former dictator could bring only dishonor on the whole nation. It was an idea that was much too painful. An untenable hypothesis. Had anyone ever heard of a country where disgrace struck every man, all of whom were guilty of not knowing how to protect their wives, daughters, sisters from a predator-tyrant? Come now! Better to hide it all under the Berber rug and behind the "taboo" banner in the name of preserving the victims' privacy. Or deny it. Label it a "nonsubject" and talk about something else. It's as simple as that. The great majority of the Guide's victims will never reveal who they are. And with good reason! As for "Gaddafi's daughters," his bodyguards, his "special service," his harem— most of whom have now fled—it's enough to describe them as loose women, as whores who basked in opulence, travel, the luxury the dictator offered them, women who as a rule have been renounced by their families. To turn them into partners of the Guide—accomplices, devoid of any morals—rather than his victims.

Denial seems to be the operating principle of Libya's current masters and offers them the advantage of their never having to deal with the nasty little secret and the great cowardice of a handful of men, formerly the dictator's indulgent valets and now zealous revolutionaries on the side of the new power. They dream of silence. Of keeping the rapes under cover. Of forgetting the women: Soraya, "Libya," Khadija, Leila, Houda, and all the others who know too much. There are so many "valiant," "heroic," "exemplary" war victims who expect and deserve gratitude and comfort from the new Libyan state. "Real" victims. Needless to say, they are men.

Let's be fair: there are some exceptions, one of whom is Mohammed al-Alagi. Meeting with him one day when all of Libya seemed hostile to me, immured in silence, boosted my energy. It was a Sunday evening in March in a café in the center of Tripoli. A taxi dropped me off after a delightful ride during which the driver had commented humorously on the caricatures of Gaddafi painted on the walls here, there, and everywhere. It was always a grotesque Gaddafi, alternately lecherous and bloodthirsty, with a disheveled clump of hair, and often disguised as a woman. "You know why?" the young man, a former rebel, asked me as I was laughing at a drawing of the dictator in a little green negligee, with a pearl necklace, false eyelashes, and scarlet red lips. "He was gay! He used to ask young guards dressed as women to dance for him." His bold language had astounded me much more than the information itself, which I'd already heard from Soraya and from a former guard at Bab al-Azizia whose young, mortified colleague had been forced to submit to this kind of session.

Mohammed al-Alagi was waiting for me with a glass of mint tea in the company of a lawyer friend. A former interim minister of justice, he is now the president of Libya's Supreme Council of Public Liberty and Human Rights, had for years been president of the Tripoli Bar Association, and had long ago won the respect of his colleagues and of foreign NGO observers with whom he communicated. Small in stature, he was wearing an English gentleman's cap above a round, sweet face with a little mustache and bright, expressive eyes. He, at least, wasn't speaking in political jargon. What a contrast after so many interviews with navel-gazing personalities, all intoxicated with their new power. "Gaddafi raped," he said. "Committed rape himself on a grand scale and ordered others to rape. Men, women. He was a sexual monster, perverse and enormously violent. I got wind of evidence of this very early on. Women lawyers, who had been raped themselves, confided in me as a friend and as a man of the law. I shared their pain but was unable to do anything. They didn't dare go to the attorney general: bringing charges would mean a death sentence. Did you see the videos online of the atrocious lynching of a few officers who had dared protest the Guide's rape of their wife? That guy was a barbarian!"

He shook his head, hunched down, both hands around his cup of boiling-hot tea. "Even during the final days of his life, hunted and helpless, he couldn't control himself. He sexually assaulted seventeen-year-old boys before the eyes of his faithful guards. No matter where, and with great brutality, too! He was cunning as a fox. And we have witnesses who confirm what he did. And I refuse to say, as some people do, that all this falls under the realm of his private life. It wasn't lovemaking—he was committing crimes. And for me rape is the most serious of all crimes."

I told him about Soraya—of the basement where she lived, her previous suffering, and her current agony. It was good to bring it to a compassionate ear. During the investigation I'd thought about her constantly. Mohammed al-Alagi listened, shaking his head. He didn't doubt the truth of what I was telling him for a moment. He found it very valuable that she had the strength to testify. "I wish we could render justice to every one of Gaddafi's victims," he said. "That would be the least we could do. It ought to be a goal for the new regime. I want investigations, public hearings, convictions, and compensation. In order to move forward, unite society, build a state, the Libyan people need to know what went on for forty-two years— hangings, torture, incarceration, mass murder, sexual crimes of all sorts. No one has any idea how much we've suffered. It's not a matter of revenge, or even of punishment. More of catharsis."

Of course, such a project would be complicated, and he didn't deny that. They were lacking in funds, structures, coordination. The government didn't know the exact number of places of detention; most of the prisons were in the hands of armed militia; and the legal system was far from being stabilized. But they needed to demand transparency—a beam of light should shine on every single crime.

It was getting very late. Al-Alagi had to leave. Speaking about Soraya, I used the word "slave" and he lost his composure. "Gaddafi thought we were all slaves! He vomited up all his past suffering over his people, destroying our culture, brushing our history aside, forcing the emptiness of the desert on Tripoli. Some Westerners swooned over his so-called culture, when really he felt nothing but contempt for knowledge and scholarship. He had to be the center of the world! Yes, he ruined Libyan society, turning his people into both victims and accomplices, and transforming his ministers into puppets and zombies. Yes, in Libya sex was an instrument of power: 'You'll shut up, you'll obey me, or I'll rape you, your wife, or your children.' And that's what he did, condemning everyone to silence. Rape was a political weapon before he made it into a military weapon."

There was such a contrast between this man and the political figures I had been able to meet. And unlike the majority of my interviewees, he wasn't afraid of being quoted by name. So we tackled the minefield of the rapes perpetrated by Gaddafi's troops during the revolution, which had taken place by the hundreds, in every town that was occupied by the dictator's militia and mercenaries. In the prisons, too. Gang rapes, committed by men who were drunk and usually on drugs, which were filmed with cell phones.

Very early on, the International Criminal Court, which had issued a warrant for the dictator's arrest in June 2011, had condemned this systematic policy of rape, but proof had been very difficult to collect and the victims couldn't be found. The women weren't talking. Physicians, psychologists, lawyers, and women's associations that wanted to come to their aid had the greatest possible trouble reaching them. So they went underground, withdrawing into their shame and sorrow. Some preferred to flee on their own terms. Others were thrown out by their families. Some were married to rebels who were willing to save the honor of these "war victims." A small number were killed by their enraged brothers. Finally, during the winter months, there were those who gave birth in great secret and immense distress.

Thanks to a network of devoted, efficient, and extremely discreet women, I was able to meet a few of these deeply traumatized women and, at the hospital, to attend some of the adoptions of babies who were the result of these rapes. These were unforgettable moments, during which the child changes hands—and its destiny—in a few seconds, and the mother, often an adolescent, is relieved but forever tormented. I also interviewed rapists in a prison in Misrata. Two pathetic guys, one twenty-two and the other twenty-nine years old, enlistees in Gaddafi's army, trembling and looking shifty as they described their crimes in detail. It was an order, they said. They were given "pills that make you crazy," and brandy and hashish, too. And their leaders would threaten them with their weapon. "Sometimes the whole family was raped. Eight- or nine-year old girls, young women of twenty, their mother, sometimes in front of a grandfather. They'd shriek, and we'd hit them hard. I can still hear their screams. I can't tell you how much they suffered. But the head of the brigade insisted: rape them, beat them up, and film it! We'll send it to their men. We know how to humiliate those bastards!"

The first one was cursing Gaddafi and begged us not to tell his mother what he was accused of having done. Tearful, the second one claimed he was eaten up with remorse and unable to find any peace. He was reading the Koran and praying day and night, had denounced all his leaders, and said he was ready for any punishment. Including death.

"The order came from very high up," Mohammed al-Alagi confirmed. "On that topic we have testimonies from those closest to Gaddafi. I myself heard Moussa Koussa, his former minister of foreign affairs, state that he had seen him order the Kataeb chiefs: 'Rape first and then kill.' It went hand in hand with his way of governing and conquering through sex." Was there any other proof needed of his strategy? Of premeditation? It was there. Hundreds of boxes of Viagra had been found in Benghazi, Misrata, Zuwarah, and even in the mountains. "They were everywhere that his militia had been stationed. And we discovered contracts of prepaid orders, signed by the 'State of Libya.' A military weapon, I told you!"

At times Muammar Gaddafi thought of himself as a writer, and in 1993 and 1994 he published sixteen short stories, full of lyrical flights of fancy, overwritten, and replete with mortifying clichés and delirious thoughts. "The stories reflected his sufferings," recalled al-Alagi, struck by the fear of the crowd that Gaddafi confessed to in *Escape to Hell,* and by how prophetic this book of short stories and essays was.

"These intemperate crowds, even towards their saviors, I feel them pursuing me . . . How affectionate they are in times of joy, holding their children high above their head. They've carried Hannibal and Pericles . . . Savonarola, Danton, and Robespierre . . . Mussolini and Nixon . . . And how cruel they are in times of anger! They plotted against Hannibal and made him drink poison, they burned Savonarola at the stake . . . sent Danton to the scaffold . . . broke Robespierre's jaws . . . dragged Mussolini's body through the streets, and spat on Nixon's face when he left the White House, although he'd been carried there on the wings of applause!"

Gaddafi added: "How I love the freedom of crowds, their enthusiasm after the chains are broken, when they burst into cries of joy and sing after moaning in pain. But how I fear and dread them! I love the multitudes the way I love my father and I fear them the way I fear him. Who, in a Bedouin society without any government, would be capable of preventing the vengeance of a father against one of his sons?"

Indeed, the crowd took vengeance. Many times during my stay in Tripoli I caught Libyans, half terrified and half fascinated, in the process of viewing the chaotic and obscene images that showed Muammar Gaddafi dying under the fighters' triumphant cries. Revolutionary songs were added to the edited scenes filmed on cell phones, an epic exultation. But there is one image the rebels didn't dare slip into most of the films. An image that two women showed me on their cell phone a few days after the Guide's death, as they placed a finger on their mouth as if it were a secret. I opened my eyes wide—the screen was tiny and the picture a little blurry. I couldn't believe it. But, yes, it was certainly there. Even before the lynching, the bodies, the bullets, the crush, a rebel violently shoved a wooden or metal stick between the buttocks of the fallen dictator, who immediately began to bleed. "Raped!" one of the two women said without an ounce of regret.

A lawyer from Misrata confirmed it. "So many Libyans felt they'd been avenged by this symbolic gesture. Before his appointment with death, the rapist was raped."

EPILOGUE

Summer returned rapidly to Tripoli, while in Paris the winter continued into an icy spring. Or so it seemed to me, at least. The sky was low and gray, the rain disheartening, and the horizon blocked. And for a brief moment every now and then, I would regret not having written this book in Libya, in the bright light, facing the Mediterranean, this story of Soraya and of Gaddafi's secret that nobody was talking about, at least not yet. The truth is that I had fled. Too much pressure, too much tension, toxic silences, poisonous confessions. I urgently needed to get some distance, reread my notebooks away from the muezzin who gave my Libyan days a rhythm with his call to prayer, which the mosque's loudspeaker would direct straight at the windows of my room.

But the distance was very relative. Even though I was in Paris while writing, my spirit remained in Tripoli and I was anxiously keeping an eye out for news from Soraya. She was probing, stumbling, becoming depressed, then picking up hope, childlike, devoid of any schedule, not knowing what to do with this past that haunted her, the terrible burden of her secret. The concept of a future didn't make any sense to her yet. Her daily obsession consisted of her cigarettes, three packs of Slims without which she couldn't live. And I angrily thought back to the scene in which the tyrant had put the first one in her mouth by force: "Inhale! Swallow the smoke! Swallow!"

Every day the Internet provided me with a sense of the Libyans' growing impatience with their temporary regime. Gasoline was flowing normally and its production was almost at the same level as before the revolution, but the people were not yet seeing any benefit. The whole country was in a state of suspense. No legitimate government, no legislators, no provincial governors, no national army, no police, no labor unions. In short, no state. Public services were in disarray, hospitals lacked equipment, and corruption was suspected everywhere. Far from being dispersed or integrated into a national structure, the militia, made up of former rebels, was reinforcing its power, declaring its own rules, and jealously guarding its prisoners in many different sites scattered throughout the region. Skirmishes between its members would occur from time to time, including the outbreak of a new kind of conflict connected to property. Ah, the wonderful Gaddafi legacy! In the late seventies, he had nationalized vast swaths of land, as well as buildings, factories, and villas. Now the former owners were appearing, armed with titles dating from the Italian occupation or the Ottoman era, and eager to immediately recover their possessions, by force if need be.

The women? They were perhaps the only ray of hope. They held their heads high, raised their voices, finally demanded a full place in society. They must have felt like they had grown wings, they were so ready to venture anything. Their participation in the revolution had been so massive that they had helped to give it legitimacy and a foundation, and they certainly intended to gather its fruits in terms of freedom, expression, and representation. They couldn't be kept out of it anymore, they thought. "It's like after the first and second world wars!" proclaimed Alaa Murabit, a brilliant medical student, raised in Canada by dissident parents, who'd come back to Libya seven years before. "The women have faced fear, risks, and responsibilities. In the absence of men, they were obliged to come out of the homes where they are frequently confined, and they have started to enjoy becoming active members of society. No more being treated like second-class citizens! We have rights. And we'll be heard!"

The Gaddafi era had opened the doors of the university to them, had provided them with military training from male instructors in high schools who broke a taboo and convinced their parents that they could work side by side with men without any undue risks. The girls had successfully taken advantage of these new educational opportunities, in medicine and law, often bringing home the highest grades. The frustration of not being able to build a prestigious career afterward had thus been all the greater. Those who intended to be a cut above the rest, aim at a prominent place, and be noticed no matter how, risked a great deal: Gaddafi and his clique of commanders, governors, and ministers were on the lookout. Were a woman to attract their attention, they would use her unscrupulously. Rapes, abductions, forced marriages . . .

"You can't imagine how afraid girls were of appearing too smart, too intelligent, too talented, or too pretty," Hana al-Galal, a lawyer from Benghazi, told me. "They would stop themselves from speaking in public. They'd relinquish illustrious posts and curtail their ambitions. They even renounced flirting, abandoned the short skirts and blouses they used to wear in the sixties to adopt the veil and loose clothing to cover their body. The golden rule was to keep a low profile. By wearing drab gray clothes, for instance—in assemblies and meetings women looked like ghosts."

That period was well and truly over. Or rather: they were hoping it was over. In post-Gaddafi Libya women are getting back in touch with their ambitions again—be they professional, economic, or political—while being quite aware that, in spite of everything, people's minds can't be changed overnight. The old guard is watchful. The proof? The famous speech given on October 23, 2011, the day that Moustapha Abdeljalil, president of the National Transition Council (CNT), officially declared that the country had been liberated. Tens of thousands of people came to attend the ceremony, which took place on the largest square in Benghazi only three days after the dictator's death. Throughout the land millions of TV screens brought together families deeply affected by the importance of the event. Libya was declaring her faith in democracy. Everyone held their breath. And without saying so, the women were waiting for a gesture, a mention of past offenses, and maybe a tribute. But it was a fiasco.

Not a word about their suffering or their contribution to the revolution. No allusion to the role they would be playing in the new Libya. Ah, yes! I forgot: a brief mention of the mothers, sisters, and daughters of the magnificent fighters to whom the country owed so much; and the announcement that, out of respect for Sharia law, henceforth the supreme reference in matters of law, polygamy would no longer be impeded by the obligation—established by Gaddafi—to ask one's first wife for permission to marry a second one. That was all. It was a slap in the face to every woman present, who from the beginning of the ceremony had been listening carefully and trying in vain to find a female silhouette on the official platform, where a host of men in suits and ties were strutting about, so proud to be embodying the takeover.

"I was shocked, furious, disgusted!" Naima Gebril, judge at the Court of Appeals in Benghazi, admitted to me a little later. "What a disastrous speech! I can assure you that it made me cry. All of that for this?" she wondered, as did so many others. "The struggle of our mothers and our grandmothers to be allowed to get an education, to get work, be respected. The energy we gave to our studies so we could triumph over discrimination and freely practice our professions. And then that complete commitment to the revolution from the first day on, while most of the men were afraid to go out. All that, just to see ourselves ignored on the day of liberation? What a disgrace!"

What a disgrace, indeed. And this is how all the women I spoke to experienced it. "Do you remember the flood of images showing the CNT [National Transition Council] delegations as they toured the Western capitals?" the first female judge of Benghazi, nominated in 1975, asked me. "Not a woman in sight!" And Hillary Clinton's visit to Tripoli, the evening before Gaddafi's capture? "Not a single Libyan woman to welcome her!" The American secretary of state had publicly taken offense at that, insisting on the need for equal rights of men and women. "How humiliating it was!" the academic Amel Jerary had said in regret. "But there you have it: no man will ever let us be in the picture or move aside to make room for us, even on the least important platform. We will have to impose ourselves by force, and I assure you that the initiatives created by women will turn out to be the most significant."

Women's alliances have been created everywhere, in the form of clubs, associations, and NGOs. These associations are grouped together in professional, amicable, regional networks. Small, clandestine cells formed during the revolution have been transformed into organizations that serve women, children, and the wounded and whose goal is further reconciliation. They have replaced masses of failing services and the government's cruel lack of initiatives. They have established internships for civic instruction to bring to mind the rights and responsibilities each woman has in a democracy: "Voting is a privilege. Use it. Now it's your turn to play!" And they are burning with desire to transform this presence in the arena into a political lobby. For they know very well that their emancipation will come only through politics.

Even a quick search on Facebook will show the abundance of Libyan women's groups, the liveliness of their discussions on the future of Libyan women, their eagerness to become informed on the situation of women in other countries of the Arab revolutions, and their desire to coordinate with these sisters as quickly as possible. Yes, they are full of hope. They comment on the plan for an electoral law, debate the appropriateness, or lack thereof, of quotas. They demand female ministers and ambassadors, directors of banks and public and administrative enterprises, affirming that they, at least, "were not molded by the Gaddafi system." Reading what they have to say is invigorating and refreshing. And I had to laugh at the picture, which they published themselves, that shows them proudly waving their new voter registration cards. And oh, yes, they certainly plan to use them!

They openly state their enthusiasm, but also admit to dispiriting moments. On May 18, a young woman I knew for her activism posted a personal and disappointed message on Facebook: "It's Friday and the weather is gorgeous. But as a woman in Libya I find myself shut away at home and depressed because I'm not allowed to go to the beach. Why are there no beaches for women? Don't we have enough shoreline? How many of you girls have the same feeling?" How many? Thousands, of course!

"It's unfair!" one of them responded.

"I lived on a street that looked out directly over the beach and wasn't even allowed to set foot there!" wrote another one.

"Totally unacceptable!"

"It's not even a matter of law. It's one of this country's tragedies!"

And this exchange:

"And yet, I still remember a time when I swam in a bikini!" . . . "A bikini? When did that change?" . . . "When a dark cloud invaded our spirits. In the middle of the seventies." . . . "We should be able to swim in bathing suits rather than in Batman outfits!"

Soraya doesn't go to the beach. She doesn't surf the Internet. She has no Facebook account. She doesn't even have any friends anymore with whom to share her angry frustrations or get registered to vote in the next elections. But she keeps hoping that Gaddafi's sexual crimes won't be forgotten. "I didn't dream it, Annick! You believe me, don't you? The names, dates, places—I've told you everything. But I really wanted to testify in a court of justice. Why should I have to be ashamed? Why do I have to hide? Why should I have to pay for the harm he did me?"

Her rebellion is mine. And I would very much have liked to share it with other Libyan women: magistrates, lawyers, those close to the CNT, defenders of individual rights. Sadly, for the time being, not one of them will wage her fight. Too sensitive. Too taboo. Nothing to be gained. Everything to lose. In a country that is entirely in the hands of men, sexual crimes will be neither debated nor judged. The people who bring up the subject will be declared insolent or deemed liars. The victims will have to remain in hiding in order to survive.

The only female member of the CNT, the lawyer Salwa el-Daghili, listened to me talk to her at length about Soraya. "How brave that little one is!" she said, shaking her head. "And it is essential that the story be known. This is the real face of the man who governed Libya for forty-two years. This is how he governed, despised, subjugated his people. We need pioneers like Soraya who dare to talk about the tragedy of women and what this country really experienced. But she runs huge risks for having spoken." She was taking notes, her face distraught under a pink headscarf, her iPhone vibrating in her Louis Vuitton bag. "The subject is taboo, they must have told you so. I hope with all my heart that Soraya is being protected. She is nothing but a victim. There are so many others. But I cannot get involved in bringing out a dossier like this."

Nobody will. And throughout the world women will continue to keep silent. Shameful victims of a crime that turns their body into an object of conquest, the spoils of war. Targets for predators toward whom our societies—from the most

285

barbaric to the most sophisticated—continue to show an appalling level of leniency.

Before leaving Tripoli in late March I wanted to take a last look at the site of Bab al-Azizia. Not much was left of what for so long had symbolized the absolute power of the master of Libya. Bulldozers had pulverized the walls, razed most of the buildings, transformed the residence into a chaotic pile of stones, cement, and sheet metal. After the final battle, hordes of people had looted the place and nothing, absolutely nothing, that might recall a human presence was left. From the dust rose mountains of trash now being handled by the population in the absence of any organized collection, and the gray palm trees shaded a swimming pool filled with brackish water. The sky was leaden, crows perched on wall remnants were surveying the place, and I was walking aimlessly over a disaster area. The landmarks one of Gaddafi's former guards had mentioned to me had been destroyed. I was lost. No matter. I moved on, trying to find a sign in this barren setting that would remind me of Soraya.

I ran into a rebel who was surveying the place—perhaps he was guarding it—and who pointed out the entrance to the basement to me. A few cement steps, an enormous red door reinforced like a safe, and a never-ending tunnel through which the man led me with his flashlight for a hundred meters or so. Climbing over a jumble of cement as we came out of the tunnel, I noticed a piece of a cassette between two stones and under a Kalashnikov. It was strange, outlandish. The title, written in Arabic, was incomplete, and the rebel explained simply: "Music!" Could it possibly be one of the tapes of syrupy songs to which Gaddafi had forced Soraya to dance? I put it in my pocket and continued the climb, then the walk. A little farther on, a crack in the floor drew my attention. Why did I stop there? There were so many of them that brought the battles of the month of August to mind or simply indicated a basement. I leaned over. At the bottom I saw a red object and was intrigued—everything else there was so gray. I couldn't work out what it was, so I grabbed a tree branch and lay down on the ground to try to hook the object onto it. It was easy: it was a piece of fabric. Out of the entrails of Bab al-Azizia came a small red lace bra. The kind of bra Soraya had been forced to wear.

For the first time since this journey had begun, I felt like weeping.

AFTERWORD

The trickle of voices has grown into an uproar. And the testimony of the outraged Libyan women that I collected in Tripoli in deepest secrecy the winter after the Revolution became a book that was sold and discussed across the globe.

Not one of us expected it, of course. Neither Soraya, who'd had trouble imagining how the account of her long ordeal in Muammar Gaddafi's harem could ever develop into the foundation of a book. Nor the handful of other women who, overcoming their terror, had confided their terrible secret to me and begged me to forget their names and telephone numbers once we'd met. Nor, finally, I myself, the journalist overwhelmed by their story, their sincerity, their trust, who felt it her duty to loudly and clearly broadcast their words, words that were unable to be heard in Libya, and turn it into an undisputed and indisputable document that might be brought before the International Criminal Court and that the new power in Tripoli wouldn't be able to ignore.

But now it is done. And at the very moment I am writing these lines, 14 February 2013, the universal day of protest of violence against women, I receive an email with two photographs of Libyan women demonstrating in a square in central Tripoli, holding up huge placards to the TV cameras, which show the cover of the book *Gaddafi's Harem*—in French and Arabic—together with banners that read NEVER AGAIN. How incredibly moving to see these images on my iPad!

Yes, the trickle of voices has grown into an uproar. The heavy silence that was Gaddafi's closest ally for forty-two years has been broken at last, and the book that will soon be discovered by American, Italian, and Chinese readers is from now on available in an Arabic translation in Libya. Shocking, indeed. A small bomb, if I dare use such a metaphor in a society saturated with weapons. It is a violation of an ancestral taboo that forbids rape and, more generally, sexuality from being openly discussed. Libya's society is the most conservative in the Maghreb. However, from the earliest rumors of the book's publication on, the new Libyan press communicated the information, dumbfounded and fascinated at the same time. In essence, the press stated that it was time for the dictator's deception to be revealed—a dictator who had dared to pose as the protector of women. His darkest crimes needed to be finally exposed. Several newspapers even called it "historic," feeling that this monstrous dossier was what was needed to open the eyes of the last fanatics. I can imagine the debates and clashes among the newspaper editors! An old guard would be shouting that it would cause a scandal, while the younger generation issuing forth from the revolutionary ranks would be delighting in breaking down the barriers. Still, as was to be expected, a number of leaders—mayors, ministers—could not hold back their disgust and shame on behalf of the whole nation. Some called for the book to be censored. Why stir up this muck again? Slap every Libyan in the face? Collectively humiliate every Libyan man? Because it was a question of male honor, once again.

But the book exists. Soraya has read it. Houda, Leila, Libya, and a few others have read it. It brings them relief. Liberates them. And torments them. How could it not? But I know they are proud to have contributed to bringing to light the truth about the man who was their torturer. In short, this was their contribution to the Revolution.

Women have so much to give in this still chaotic country that dreams of joining the free world and, feverishly and furiously, is trying to reinvent itself.

Annick Cojean
14 February 2013

CHRONOLOGY

1911: Beginning of the Italian occupation of Libya

1943–1951: International trusteeship

1951: Proclamation of the State of Libya, monarchy of King Idris I

1969: Coup d'état by Colonel Gaddafi, twenty-seven years old

1976: Publication of the *Green Book*

1977: Proclamation of the Jamahiriya, literally the "State of the Masses"

1986: American raid on the residences of Gaddafi in Tripoli and Benghazi

1988: Pan Am's Boeing 747 explodes above Lockerbie, Scotland

1989: UTA's DC-10 explodes above Niger

2001: Gaddafi's new positioning against terrorism the day after September 11

2004: Partial lifting of American and European sanctions

February 17, 2011: Beginning of the revolution

October 20, 2011: Capture and death of Gaddafi

AUTHOR'S ACKNOWLEDGMENTS

This investigation owes a great deal to the commitment of a courageous, independent, and passionate Libyan woman. A rebel leader who was committed heart and soul to the revolution from the first day on, and who took many risks to transport weapons, fighters, civilians, and wounded across a Libya at war. A heroine of great integrity, determined to discreetly and efficiently come to the aid of Libya's most vulnerable, most distraught women, who suffered the most hateful crimes, perpetrated or ordered by Gaddafi himself, and still only barely acknowledged by her country. A woman who, despite pressure and threats, continues to devote herself to the cause of women. I express my gratitude toward her here.

I have had the good fortune to work—for thirty years now, since time immemorial—at a newspaper to which I am deeply attached and that has granted me both the time and the trust to make this project a reality. My gratitude goes to those in charge of *Le Monde*.

ABOUT THE TRANSLATOR

Born in Indonesia, raised in the Netherlands, and residing in the USA, Marjolijn de Jager translates from the French and the Dutch. She is retired from a lengthy career in teaching French and Francophone language and literature, and translation is now her full-time occupation, with Francophone African literature occupying a special place in her heart. Among her honors are an NEA grant, two NEH grants, and, in 2011, the annually awarded ALA Distinguished Member Award, received from the African Literature Association for scholarship, teaching, and translations of African literature. For further information, please see mdejager.com.